Minimalist Budget:

Powerful Strategies of Financial Budgeting. Save Money, Improve Bad Debt, Avoid Emotional Spending and Learn Money Management

2

any kind are declared or implied. Readers acknowledge that the author is not engaging in the rendering of legal, financial, medical or professional advice. The content within this book has been derived from various sources. Please consult a licensed professional before attempting any techniques outlined in this book.

By reading this document, the reader agrees that under no circumstances is the author responsible for any losses, direct or indirect, which are incurred as a result of the use of information contained within this document, including, but not limited to, — errors, omissions, or inaccuracies.

Table of Contents

Introduction

I would like to thank you for purchasing this book

What is a minimalist budget? How do you apply the philosophy of minimalism to your finances? Another thing that you might want to ask is if such a budget works. All of these questions and more will be answered in this book.

Minimalism is centered on the idea of "less is more." You live with less and are not burdened by the pressures of our modern living, which focuses on the accumulation of material possessions.

When you look at people who live a minimalist lifestyle you will see them in homes with wide-open spaces, very little clutter, not pressured by social media, and content with owning the things that they already have.

They're unaffected by fads. You don't see them rushing to the next sale. They even manage their finances very well. They don't even max out their credit cards—they still use them, and they can manage their debt very well.

In short, you don't see the usual excesses that our commercialized way of living has promoted these many decades. A minimalist budget emphasizes getting the best quality things and gaining more life experiences instead of focusing on just obtaining possessions.

With that kind of philosophy, you can already see at the onset that a minimalist life can free up your finances. Sure, you're still shopping online and are mindful of the latest trends. But you don't get pressured when your friends egg you into buying the latest gizmo in town.

You Can't Have a Minimalist Budget without Being a Minimalist

Yes, you can't use a minimalist budget without becoming a minimalist to a certain degree. You can't apply this budget and still, be on the lookout for the next upcoming sale for your 11th dishwasher and still keep the other 10 in your house.

You can't expect a minimalist budget to help you financially if you're still spending money on things that you don't really need.

Don't expect a minimalist budget to save your finances if you're still buying things impulsively. These two things—impulsive buying and minimalism—just don't mix.

Can you be a semi-minimalist, say apply it to your budget and still collect certain things? You can, but you at least need to have a degree of self-control when it comes to how you spend your money.

You also need to specifically identify the items you want to collect and you have quit being an "I gotta have that by hook or by crook" sort of person.

However, once you experience the benefits of minimalism in your finances, you are already a few steps away from being a complete minimalist and living that kind of lifestyle.

Chances are when all is said and then, you can easily see the benefits of minimalist living and you will end up being a minimalist as well in the long run.

What are the Benefits?

Minimalism when applied to your financial life brings with it a host of benefits. They include the following:

- Being free of the usual financial worries
- Getting rid of financial clutter (e.g. unwanted expenses, impulsive spending)
- Get more life experiences
- Getting more quality possessions

- Live a greener life
- Reduce stress
- Be free of debt
- Foster better relationships with people who matter

What We Will Cover in This Book?

If you found these benefits as something truly desirable—things that you want to have in your life, then the tips, instructions, and ideas in this book could be quite helpful to you. In this book we will go through a lot:

- What is a minimalist budget?
- Samples of minimalist budgets (yes, you can create your own)
- How to formulate a minimalist budget that works best for you
- How to set limits on your spending
- How to live a minimalist and still maintain your social life
- How do avoid financial distractions
- Using budget plans
- The secret financial formula for budgeting success
- Why is spending emotionally driven and how can you master your emotions

- Minimalist tests and rules that will help you get more with less
- How to grow and manage your savings
- Tools that you can use to manage and save money
- How to deal with bad debt

This is book 1 of a 2 part book series. This book focuses on minimalist budgeting and how you can use it in your life right now. Book 2 is all about getting out of debt and staying out of debt.

Both of these books were written with the intent of telling my experience and the lessons I learned after making a lot of financial mistakes. If you find the ideas that are covered in these pages beneficial to you right now, then read on.

Once again, thanks for purchasing this book, I hope you find it to be helpful!

Chapter 1: What is a Minimalist Budget?

What is a minimalist budget? Another thing that you might want to ask is if such a budget works. When applied to one's finances, minimalism simply means the application of "having less is more" to the money matters in life.

That means you will impose limits on your purchases—for some these limits can be more drastic than others. The change will depend on each individual's spending habits.

The goal of a minimalist budget is to reduce one's spending to the bare minimum or as close to it as possible. It also means spending your hard-earned money on things that are necessary first and the things that you want, well, maybe later if ever.

It's Not Exactly About Being Cheap or Frugal

Using a minimalist budget isn't necessarily the cheaper alternative. On the contrary, for some people, it might even translate to spending more money than they used to. Now, what is that you say?

The focus on minimalism isn't just in smaller quantities. Apart from avoiding habits of spending frivolously on items that you don't really need, minimalism inspires spending on real quality things.

You don't sacrifice quality, you just let go of the quantity of your purchases. So for instance, you used to own a collection of countertop juicers—everything from a cheap buck ninety unknown brands to some fancy high tech $100 masticating Breville juicer, you will have to sell both of these items in your next garage sale.

What you might have to do is to purchase a better quality $400 highly durable Omega juicer. At least you have covered part of that cost when you sold your other juicers in your garage sale.

As you can see, when you switch to a minimalist budget you are essentially investing in better quality albeit more expensive and pricier items.

You're looking to purchase things that will last and items that serve you the best.

However, having said that, since the focus of minimalism is on quality—it is also possible to live a minimalist budget and make significant savings as well. Remember, quality doesn't always translate into pricey things.

There is a way to live with a minimalist budget and practicing frugality. Again, the focus is on quality and nothing more.

The Functions of a Minimalist Budget

I have seen friends cringe when someone mentions the word "budget" in our discussions. Budgets and budgeting have sometimes had a bad rap in certain circles but it takes some real experience before you realize that it is something essential.

Some people I have spoken to complain that it is impossible to stick to a budget, that you can't control your spending. In short, they say that life happens and when it does it can ruin any budget.

Someone once said that using a budget is burdensome. Your mind is already weighed down by a lot of things, then why should one bother doing the math day in and day out just to make sure that your spending is within certain limits.

There are even those who say that using a budget fosters a mindset of scarcity.

Well, please allow me to summarize all of their arguments in one statement—what they are essentially trying to say is that ***budgets don't work***.

Unfortunately, **such a sentiment is misguided at best**. If budgets don't work then why do multibillion-dollar industries use budgets? Why do world governments use budgets? Centuries of experience tells us that the smartest and the richest folks on earth use budgets.

However, we should also carefully point out that ***a budget is merely a tool***. When it is used properly, it can bring the results that you may be looking for.

Here's something from my own personal experience:

When I was in my mid-20s I was in debt—it is a modest estimate at best—to put it simply, I wasn't making enough money to cover for everything. A friend of mine who was kind enough to give me advice gave me some budgeting tips.

The idea was simple and should have been a no-brainer from the start but I was skeptical. I always thought that I can always work hard and make enough money for myself and pay for everything.

I will share with you his simple strategy in a later chapter. For now, I'll just let you in on the core of the ideas and concepts that he shared—it was minimalism. The gist of the tactics and strategy that he shared centered on the idea of living within your means and accepting that less is more.

Here are the things that I was able to do within the two and a half years of applying his budgeting strategy:

- I was able to pay off $50,000 in debt, including some remaining student loans
- I was able to invest thousands of dollars that allowed me to generate passive income over time.
- I was able to save up to six months worth of what used to be my unnecessary expenses (this went into an emergency fund that I can go to in case I lost my job or something)
- I was able to buy my very first car (nothing fancy but it wasn't a jalopy either)

Not bad for a salaried man, right? You see, a minimalist budget has two functions, which includes the following:

1. It makes you mindful about your spending habits

2. It also helps you ensure that you stay within spending limits

If you don't have those two things you can be spending too much money on things that you don't really need and you could also be spending the money you haven't yet earned (using credit cards, loans, etc.).

Use Percentages of Your Monthly Income

This is a concept that I have personally experimented on and I know that it works. It will help you achieve the two functions of budgets and budgeting mentioned earlier. Use certain percentages of your monthly income on several things that should be part of your budget plan.

Remember that you can adjust the percentages as you identify any unnecessary spending that you have been habitually doing. Let's say you discover that you are wasting money on a $10 latte first thing in the morning.

You don't need that expensive coffee so you decide that you can live without it. You will then compute what percentage of your budget goes to that and then reassign that amount to some other category.

To simplify things we'll just include a few general categories. In a later chapter, we will deal with the specific parts of a budget. For now, let's say you want to categorize your expenses into:

1. Needs
2. Wants
3. Savings

You need to decide how much of your budget should go into your savings, how much of that should go into your needs, and how much of that monthly income should go into your wants.

You can formulate things simply as:

1. 20% for savings
2. 50% for needs
3. 30% for wants

So, when you get your pay each month, 20% of that should be taken out and placed in a savings fund. Your savings should be used for emergencies, investments, or any big-ticket expense like maybe a wedding or a new car.

You can open a new bank account and put all those savings there. The idea here is to pay yourself first. We'll go into the details of why paying yourself first is an effective strategy a little later.

You should then spend 50% of your monthly income on your needs like food, rent, gas, etc. And finally, you should take out 30% of your monthly income and spend it on your wants—you can on a date, go to a spa, get fancy dinners, etc.

IMPORTANT NOTE: remember that these percentages aren't always fixed. There are months when these values will fluctuate—everything will depend on your current circumstances. Sometimes you will have to reduce the amount you have allocated for your wants and put them into your needs—let's say you got sick and you had to pay for medical bills for example.

RULE OF THUMB: if you have to make adjustments to these percentages, you should reduce the amount for your wants first, needs second, and savings last. As much as possible, you should make sure that your savings money will always remain intact. It is the money that you expect to "save" you from financial trouble in the future.

Light Budgeting

Let's say you're new to budgeting and all those percentages are just too confusing for now. Here's something that you can use to start with. After you get comfortable using this strategy, you can switch to the previous method described earlier.

With the light budgeting scheme all you have to do is to classify all the expenses that you make into two distinct categories:

1. Fixed Expenses
2. Variable Expenses

Fixed Expenses: These are things that you pay for each month that rarely changes. Expenses that fall into this category include rent, student loan payments, power bills, water bills, insurance, phone bill, etc.

Variable Expenses: These are expenses that usually change depending on how much you need or want them. They include your expenditure on food and groceries, dates, entertainment, etc.

So, how do you do this budget? The first step is to compute the total monthly fixed expenses that you pay for. Determine how much is your monthly rent, add to that your phone bill, water bill, power bill, monthly student loan payments, etc.

Once you have determined how much you have to pay each month, take that money out and make all the payments as soon as you can. The rest of the money then goes to whatever it is you want to spend it on.

It's simple, right?

However, with regard to your variable expenses—you should spend money on food and other supplies first. You can then spend what's left on stuff that you like to spend on.

So, let's say you earn $2,000 a month. You pay $1,000 on rent, cellphone, loans, etc. so you take that out first and pay all the bills you have to pay. You determine that your food and essentials cost you $400 each month so you use that much money for that.

The remaining $600 is something that you can spend at will. When that money runs out, you're not supposed to spend a dollar more.

The "No Budget" System

This is probably the simplest budget of the three basic budgets that I have learned. Note, however, that this may not be the best option for people like me who tend to do some impulse buying from time to time.

It may be called a "no budget" system, but don't let that fool you. You will still be using a budget albeit a rather over-simplified one.

The no-budget system goes like this:

When you get your salary for this month, take out 20% and put it in your savings fund. Whatever is left, you can spend at will. There is no need for expense tracking, no need for a complex set of categories to monitor, nothing.

The danger with this method is that you are not monitoring anything. Sure, you have set aside some savings. But you don't monitor how much you have already spent on bills, and your wants.

If you're not mindful enough, you may have already spent too much on food, drinks, and partying, that you forgot that you haven't paid your rent. You may no longer have enough money for gas or your phone bill.

Sometimes people who use this method run out of money before they get their next pay. This method is for people who have more control over their spending. If you're usually a frugal kind of guy who can prioritize your needs before your wants, then this simple budgeting strategy might work well for you.

I recommend the first two strategies for absolute beginners. The third option should be used by those who have better budgeting skills and those who can avoid impulse buying.

A Final Word for This Chapter

Note that the basic budgeting strategies described earlier are meant for you to practice how to use and follow a budget. We will fine-tune your spending and budgetary practices as we go on with the other ideas, tips, and techniques that will be explained later on.

Key Takeaways

Here are the key points that you have learned in this chapter:

1. A minimalist budget is one that focuses on quality and not quantity
2. A minimalist budget allows you to monitor your spending habits and set limits on the amount of money you spend. It takes a lot of self-control and self-monitoring but it can be done.
3. A budget is merely a tool—how you use this tool will dictate your success or failure

4. For starters, you can try three basic budgeting methods or systems, which are: monthly income percentages, light budgeting, and the "no budget" system.
5. You can formulate your own minimalist budget.

What You Can Do

Choose either the income percentages budgeting method or the light budgeting method and try that out for one month. Determine how much money you are able to save that will carry over to the next month.

The goal is to secure at least a little amount of savings for that month when you tried any of these budgeting tactics.

It is important that you try any kind of budgeting. That is a lot better than having no budget at all.

It may not be a minimalist budget yet, but we'll get to that. The goal is to start getting into the habit of budgeting your money. You can then tweak your budget later on so that you can put minimalist principles into practice with your financial affairs.

Chapter 2: How to Get Started on a Minimalist Budget

We have outlined what a minimalist budget is and we have also provided several simple examples of what these budgets would look like. We need to emphasize at this point that a minimalist budget will help you gain financial clarity by reducing the clutter in the money matters of your life.

The good news is that a minimalist budget is not rocket science. It is all about simplification of your finances so you will have more time and money so you can be more financially free.

How to Get Started

Minimalism applied to your finances will simplify things but *that doesn't mean you will always be spending less* on everything. There will be times when you will spend more money because *you are after the quality of an item or service.*

In short, minimalism applied to money matters is more about getting more out of your money even though you end up buying fewer things. There will be times when you will be frugal and there will be times when you will have to splurge a bit.

The emphasis here, again as a reminder, is on the quality of things.

This means that minimalism will allow you to still use your credit cards. However, you will also be intentionally looking for ways to maximize your credit card use and not just mindlessly buying anything you see on sale.

You will be looking for the best deals and, coupon offers, and rewards hack. Because of this, a minimalist budget can help you straighten out your finances, simplify your purchasing decisions, manage your money, and achieve your financial goals.

There are a few guiding principles that you should know about so you can get started on a minimalist budget. These will guide you in your decisions as you transition to a minimalist mindset and lifestyle.

Establish Your Own Financial Priorities and Values

The first step to using a minimalist budget is to define your financial values as well as your financial priorities. After establishing both things, you will then be able to identify what is necessary to you and which one is unnecessary.

If you are not able to judge what is essential to your finances and which ones aren't then you won't be able to identify your needs and wants. Here's what you should do:

1. Identify what things you value financially
2. Identify which items you spend on are actually essential to you
3. Identify things that are nice to have but not absolutely necessary – things that can make life more comfortable/improve the quality of life.
4. Identify things that you purchase that are on the fringes—they're not really necessary and they don't necessarily improve the quality of your life.

Things that are Financially Valuable to You

People value different things especially when it comes to their finances. Some people value the security of getting that paycheck each month. Others value the sanctity of real property. Others prefer the play on risk and trading stocks, bonds, and other financial instruments.

Some people value retiring early in life, others value earning their first million dollars, while still others value the solidarity of establishing a million-dollar enterprise. It is different for everybody.

Here are some examples of financial values that you might want to consider as you formulate your minimalist budgeting strategy:

- Retire by age 50
- Donating 10% of your income to your church or a charity of your choice
- Have a 40% buffer fund that you can use during tough times
- Save at least 20% of your income each month
- Have a sizable retirement fund that will allow you to live a comfortable (or maybe

a luxurious) life by the time you quit working

- Be totally free of debt

Your list of financial values will be different from what others have. It will be unique in some way. The values that you will have in this list will determine what your priorities are financially.

These values will also determine what your priorities are and they will affect the decisions that you will make. Again, this list is a tool and it will help you decide on things especially when times get rough.

Your values will help you determine your financial goals and you will know how to achieve financial freedom just like the way you want it. Here's my own list of goals after I determined my financial values—they're listed in chronological order:

1. Pay off all my debts, including student loans, credit cards, mortgage, etc. within 4 years.
2. After all my debt is paid start a substantial lifeline fund for emergencies that is equivalent to 12 months of my salary.
3. Donate 10% of my income to the church

4. Increase my income by 20% by looking for side jobs or by making small investments
5.   Add 5 steady income streams in the next 5 years
6. Retire by age 55

You don't have to follow my list of financial goals and you don't have to copy any of my financial values. These are all subjective choices that everyone must make depending on the things they want out of life.

There are many different ways you can establish your own financial priorities. If you're a bit unsure about how you will go about it, then try answering this question:

What is the value of experiences to you compared to the value of things?

Some people value things like houses, cars, and other property. However, some people value experiences like vacations, training, special moments that are spent with friends and loved ones, vacations, trips to other parts of the world, and other experiences. Studies show that people tend to be happier when they spend their hard earned money on experiences than on property.

But that doesn't mean you can't spend money on both. The important thing is that you are able to choose the things that you truly value in life. However, if you want to feel that you have spent your money well, then you should spend more of it on gaining life experiences.

Prioritize those over other things then you will be set for life.

Remember that you need to set your financial priorities if you want to create a minimalist budget. This is one of the foundations of minimalism as it applies to one's finances.

What You Should Do: Make a list of things that you value financially. And then edit and fine-tune that list so that it becomes a list of the priorities you want to do with your money in the long run.

You can separate the list into short term and long term priorities. You should also assign a monetary value for each item. For example, how much do you want to spend on your new home, how much for that vacation to the pacific, how much do you want as a retirement fund.

Make sure that these priorities are the things that you really want in life.

Switch to an Ownership Mindset

There is a very common financial trap that is laid out for people who have a poor man's mindset. They would usually purchase items with payment terms that will stretch out the number of payments for a number of years.

You may have heard of deals like a car with lease payments as low as $200 a month or something similar. These payments will allow you to make the lowest payments available. And of course, you will pay interest on the term of the lease of the car.

Do you see the trap here?

Sure you're making small payments each month and you get to enjoy the car right away. It's instant gratification, right? What people don't see is that they are actually buying something that is actually above and beyond what their salaries can afford.

If you compute the total amount that you will have paid over the years of all your term payments, you will have paid for more than double the original purchase price of the car (or whatever item it is you're buying).

Sure, you already have the car when you make your down payment. It makes you feel entitled and perhaps empowered. However, what you don't see is that you are already living beyond your means and the fact is that you really can't afford the car you think you have bought.

Think Ownership

Switching to a minimalist budget will require you to have a paradigm shift. Instead of looking at the enticement (i.e. the low monthly payment terms), you need to think in terms of actual ownership of the item you want to buy.

Instead of asking how much the monthly payments are, what you should be asking is how much you will have to pay for the car outright. When you purchase that way, you will not only gain full ownership of the car, the seller will also be willing to give you a good discount for the sale.

You may have made a huge one-time purchase by paying for the car outright, but in the long run, you are actually saving a lot of money.

The Financial Mindfulness Paradigm Shift

The shift in mindset may or may not include the use of credit cards. But if you are a mindfulness advocate and own a credit card, expect to use your credit card only for essential purchases.

You will also use your credit card to its fullest potential—that doesn't mean you will max it out. That means you will take advantage of deals that may come along such as zero interest rates and fair discount offers.

Being mindful of your purchases and practicing minimalism doesn't always mean being absolutely frugal—as in our example of purchasing a car outright. However, by mastering your finances, you will realize that your income potential is rather limitless.

You don't need a credit review to tell you how much you can buy or how much you're worth. You can figure that out for yourself because you can buy quality premium items out of your own pocket. You don't need a bank or any other financial institution to give you a loan to make that purchase.

The goal here is to be mindful of every purchase that you will make. Instead of impulsively buying things in cash or on credit, you will take a minute to consider what you're buying and the emotions you are experiencing at the moment. We will go back to this principle several times in this book as we scrutinize the details of minimalism and mindfulness as they are applied to one's budget.

We will also go over some exercises and techniques to help you become more mindful about spending money.

Formulate a Minimalist Budget

How do you exactly formulate your own minimalist budget? The first step is to identify all the recurring monthly costs. And then from there, you move on to your spending habits. It's a very simple step by step process that you can follow and it is outlined below.

Step 1: Set Your Minimalist Goals

Again, as it was explained earlier, you need to start with your goals. In this section, I would like to share with you a bit about my story. I will also share several ways you can remember and keep to the goals that you have set for yourself.

Earlier we mentioned that you can't use a minimalist budget without practicing at least a small amount of minimalistic philosophy and lifestyle. We all know that a budget is crucial if you want your financial plan to be a success.

However, like many folks have found out through the years, a budget is not an easy thing.

If you have tried the budgeting strategies that we have discussed in the previous chapter, you will notice one thing:

Budgeting is hard, right?

Sticking to your budget can be a really tough cookie. Come on, you have to admit it after trying at least one kind of budgeting strategy. Creating a budget is one thing, but getting started with it and sticking to it is a totally different animal.

The temptations you have to beat just to be able to stick to your budget—especially in my case (case in point: I'm an impulsive buyer!)—it can easily turn into a horrendous experience.

Apart from the temptation to spend the money you have on you, you also have a lot of things to think about: groceries, savings, debts, your kid's tuition, your mortgage, car payments. The list goes on and on and on.

So, how do you keep things together?

The solution is to learn more about minimalism and minimalist philosophy and then set your minimalist goals.

In my experience, one of the best ways I was able to curb my impulsive spending was to make it my goal to spend my money only on worthwhile things.

Now, I had to be specific coz the mind can play tricks on you and you can rationalize anything on sale as "something worth my while." So, I had to establish certain categories of expenses as *worthwhile* things.

I had the following when I first started. Of course, that changed as I learned more about what I really wanted in life. My goals also changed from time to time:

1. Save for retirement
2. Pay my debts and create an emergency fund
3. Things that let me learn a new skill or create a life experience that will build my character
4. Investment in my physical and mental well being

Now, even though these minimalist goals were in their infancy, they helped me a lot.

How did all that help me?

Here's how. Whenever I am tempted to buy something, I look at that list of worthwhile things—well, more like categories of things that should be worthwhile for me.

So, when the latest iPhone came out, I had to stop and think. I had some money I could spend on a new phone. Yes, I still have the old one and it works quite alright.

I then ask myself if buying the next iPhone going to help me save for retirement? Will that purchase help me save rainy day money or pay my debt? Will buying that phone help to build my character? Is it an investment in my mental or physical well-being?

Guess what. The answer to all of those questions was a big NO. So, I ended up stopping myself from buying the new iPhone that was advertised on the internet, the TV, and pretty much everywhere you look in town.

Now, your goal doesn't have to be the same as my goal. I just used that as an example that I hope you can relate with.

Pick your own goals. It can be setting money aside for that dream vacation, get enough money for a sizable emergency fund, save cash that you can use for Christmas and the holidays; get a new car… it can be anything.

Remembering Your Goals

The next step is to use something to remind you of this goal. Some guys use a ring, necklace, a watch, and a particular haircut, a note written on a small piece of paper that is within easy reach, a catchphrase, a mantra, or even a simple gesture like a pat on the wrist.

What you need is a physical reminder—something that you perceive through your senses—so that you not only engage your mind,

36

you also involve your senses and trigger emotions.

The important thing here is that you can use these goals as a reminder. Whenever you get the urge to spend outside of your intended budget, you use those reminders

Minimalist methods to keep you reminded of your goals:

- ***Clean up your desktop screen and use the background picture as your reminder***: one way to practice minimalism is to do it in the digital sense. First, remove all the unnecessary apps and icons on your desktop—I mean on your computer and on your phone as well. The goal is to allow you to see what's on your wallpaper. Now, change your wallpapers to the pictures of your chosen goal. Now, every time you look at your phone or computer, you will be reminded of your goals.

- ***Use your screen saver or lock screen***: do this on both your phone and on your computer. Change the screen saver or lock screen into a picture of your goal. For example, if your goal is to travel to Italy, then put a picture of some famous place in Italy where you want to go to.

- ***Set an alarm using one of your goals as your reminder text:*** one alarm will do, and I would like to suggest that you set the timer right smack in the middle of the most stressful hours of your day—mine was at 10 am in the office (i.e. during workdays). I needed to be reminded of my goals so I don't walk out for a coffee break to spend $15 on an overly expensive cup of coffee.

- ***Use reminder browser extensions:*** set these reminders or browser extensions to bug you (i.e. remind you) of your goals. I have set mine to go off at the end of my shift. That way I end my workday on a good note and I get reminded not to go on a stress shopping trip.

- ***Written reminders:*** written reminders are a bit of a standard so I decided to just throw it in this list. You can use post its, notes on the fridge, whiteboards, corkboards, sticky notes on the mirror, your car's steering wheel, on top of the

TV, your wallet, and other everyday places that you will likely check. The goal here is to associate the reminder with the things that you do every day so that they will be easier to recall. Never over-do written reminders though or else you'll end up with a lot of clutter all over your home and place of work.

- **Unwritten reminders**: you should use unwritten reminders after you have used written reminders. The unwritten ones will require more effort and practice before you can make full use of them. What you can do is to associate the things you see every day with your goals. For instance, you can associate your financial goals with everyday objects like your watch, your wallet, or even with just a song. I had a friend who found the Travie McCoy/Bruno Mars song "Billionaire" quite helpful.

- **Have an Accountability Partner**: we will go over the details of what an accountability partner is and what he or she can do for you a little later in this book. For now, just remember that an accountability partner is someone that you can trust with the current state of your finances. One of the roles of this person is to help you remember your financial goals especially when you're tempted to spend money outside of your budget. Every time you feel tempted to spend money on something that you don't really need, you can call or send a message to this person and he can offer support and remind you of your goals.

Step 2: Identifying Your Monthly Recurring Costs

The first step in creating your own minimalist budget is to identify your MRC or recurring monthly costs. Yes, that is a billing term and you will usually hear that from your customer service person from Verizon or some other telco.

When we say MRC we refer to more than just your monthly phone bill. These include static costs and any other expense that you need to pay each month without fail. If you fail to pay them, then there will be serious financial consequences.

The consequences come in the form of surcharges, fees, or even disconnection or discontinuation of services. They are not discretionary—you can't skip paying this month and hope you will still do fine without them.

In short, you really have to pay them—period. Here is a list of monthly recurring costs that you can include in your budget:

- **Housing**

Housing costs can be your rent, if you live in an apartment or if you're renting a house. It can also be your mortgage. This cost will vary significantly depending on where a person lives.

The median home value in Ohio, for instance, is around $141,000. But that will go up to around $328,000 if the home was bought in New Jersey. You can hire a professional to compute that for you or you can use the cost of living calculators, which you can find online.

The average household in the USA spends around $1,700 each month on housing. This estimate is from the Department of Labor. The estimated average income is around $6,500 (i.e. it may have changed recently, so this is just an estimate as of the writing of this book). Given these figures, your housing costs will make up the bulk of your MRC.

- **Emergency Fund**

Some people consider savings as just that – "savings." However, here's a secret when it comes to minimalist budgeting—consider every dollar you put into savings as an expense. That way you pay yourself first before anything else. We'll go into that a little later in this book.

So, how much of an emergency fund should be your goal? Best practice dictates that you should make it your goal to have at least 6 months' worth of expenses as your emergency fund.

If it is possible, every payday you should set aside 10% of your income towards that emergency fund. Keep doing that until your emergency fund totals to 6 months of monthly expenses.

Note that 6 months is a rather conservative projection. Given the many financial distresses that we have experienced through the years (e.g. pandemic, stock market crash, recessions, etc.), I would suggest that you make your emergency fund around 12 months' worth of your monthly expenses.

That way, if a recession goes on for an extended period, you have an entire year to find a way to focus your efforts on finding financial opportunities.

So let's say you spend $2,000 a month as your total monthly expenses. Your goal will be to save around a three-month equivalent, which would be $12,000 as your rainy day or emergency fund.

If you set aside $2,000 each month, then you will have $24,000 as your emergency fund after 12 months.

Sometimes that will be too overwhelming—especially if you're already facing a lot of financial challenges at the moment. I totally understand that. That is why I suggest that you set aside 10% of your monthly income towards your emergency fund.

It may take you longer than 12 months to save the total amount for your emergency fund, but at least you have money that you can use in case something unexpected happens, right?

- **Retirement Fund**

Here's a big life lesson that should be ingrained in you right now—and fast: no one else is going to pay for your retirement other than you yourself. Don't expect the government to help you out.

Don't expect your friends and family to help you when you're old and retired. That is why you should be working towards saving for your retirement now. The earlier you can do this, the better.

Why? This is because your retirement fund can benefit longer from the power of compounding interest. I would suggest that you set aside 10% to 15% of your monthly income for your retirement.

Do that religiously.

If you can save well enough for your retirement, then you will have enough funds kept for yourself even if an economic downturn comes along in the future.

- **Credit Card Debt**

Now, this is one monthly recurring cost that a lot of people are keenly aware of. So, how much should you pay each month for your credit card debt? It may be a bit difficult, but if you can manage 10% of the total balance in your debt, then do it.

Here's a simple yet rough estimate: let's say your credit card balance is around $5,000. And let's say that you are paying 15% interest. By paying $500 each month, you can pay off your entire credit card bill in a year.

- **Student Loans**

Back in 2018, it was reported that 75% of students had student loans that they had to pay after graduation. Chances are you may have incurred some form of student loans. You should work out the amounts of the monthly term payments that you need to pay in order to be free of these loans.

For example, let's say you need to pay $29,000 in student loans (the average back in 2018); you plan to pay that loan in five years with 6%

interest. You need to make an estimated $570 payment each month for five years. That's how much you need to set aside as a monthly recurring cost.

Remember that's just an example. Your monthly figures for your student loan payments will be different.

- **Insurance**

Another monthly cost that you may have to pay is insurance. This includes life insurance, home insurance, pet insurance, auto insurance, and others. I'm not saying that you need to have all of that insurance but whatever insurances you have each month needs to have a specific budgeted amount set aside for it too.

- **Food and Other Necessities**

Food and other necessities are obviously something that you need to spend month after month. You may also include transportation and utility bills here too if you want.

Step 3: Evaluate Your Spending Habits

After identifying your monthly costs, the next step is to determine your spending habits. You need to discover how you spend your money from day-to-day. This will be a huge eye-opener for some people. By tracking your spending habits, you will find out what your variable expenditures are.

To determine your spending habits, answer the following questions:

- How much do you pay on average for each meal?
- How often do you dine out?
- How often do you go shopping?
- How much shopping money did you spend this month?
- How often do you buy shoes and clothing?
- Do you indulge in hobbies from time to time? How much do you spend on each hobby?
- How often do you go to the bar? How much do you spend there on average?
- How often do you go to the movies? How much do you spend for that?
- How much do you spend for drinks, snacks, coffee, etc.?
- How often do you order stuff online?
- How many streaming services do you subscribe to?

After computing that, you can now discover how you spend your money each month. Add the amount you spend for your monthly fixed costs (step number 2) to the total amount you have for your variable spending (step number 3).

We will go over the many different ways you can cut back on spending in chapter 4 of this book.

Step 4: Set Spending Limits

If you want to control your spending and go by a minimalist budget, then you have to set spending limits. This step will also allow you to save some money each month as well.

At the moment you may see that you aren't able to save very little if any at all. But don't worry, with careful planning and following a minimalist budget, you will see some definitive improvement overtime.

Here are a few ideas that you can do when you make that inventory:

- ***Determine how much you want to spend for each expense category*** – how much do you think should be your budget for food and supplies? How much do you think should spend on gas and other utilities? You make this initial estimate first and then make adjustments

47

as you go over the next step, which is making an inventory of your belongings.

- ***Make an inventory of all your belongings*** – take stock of everything you have. This is one of the first things that you will usually do to live a minimalist lifestyle. You will be decluttering your home. Through this process, you might even realize how much you really have.

  Evaluate each item and everything that you don't really need or things you haven't used for the past 1 to 2 years should either be given to charity or sold on eBay or in a garage sale.

  Of course, if you aren't working towards a minimalist lifestyle and you're just after a minimalist budget (yes, as I mentioned earlier, you can have a minimalist budget without going 100% on minimalist living), then you can skip the selling and giving away to charity part.

  At the very least, you make an inventory of your possessions. Reorganize and categorize your belongings. Next time you feel like you want to spend money on something (e.g. clothes, gadgets, etc.), you can come back to this inventory and determine whether you already have a lot of that type of item or not.

Say, you see a new laptop model, but then you notice that you already have like six gaming laptops—you can then decide whether you really need that new laptop or not. You can then make a choice, whether the new model is worth buying in which case you will have to either sell or give away the older laptops or just stick with what you have. Remember, again, minimalist budgeting is more about quality over quantity.

- ***Separate Wants from Needs*** – you might want some cake for dessert after every meal. However, the question is do you really need it? You feel tempted to buy that new suit—do you want it or do you need it?

Of course, you can't paint everything in black and white. You can even argue everything either way. For instance, let's talk about a gym membership. You can argue that going to the gym is definitely a necessity because it can help you keep fit. You're staying healthy because of that gym membership so, you can argue that it is definitely a need and not a want.

However, check out what kind of gym membership it is in the first place. If it is a luxury membership worth $200, then you have to ask if that is a need or a want. Maybe you can go to a less expensive gym but also get the same health benefits and quality workout. You get health and fitness and you save money—a great win/win.

- ***Look for Excesses in Your Spending*** – there will usually be excesses in our spending especially when you always go over your budget each month. This is one of the ways you can fine-tune any kind of budget whether it is a minimalist one or not. Your budget isn't working for you because you are not looking into the finer details.

  For example, do you often throw away a lot of spoiled or wasted food? That should be an indicator that you are wasting money on groceries and other food items. Go over your inventory and the list of expenses that you have outlined in the previous steps.

You have made initial spending limits as the first step, right? Now, after doing an inventory, separating your wants from your needs, you will have to decide whether your initial estimates were correct or do they need an adjustment.

Let's say you initially set 2 thousand dollars as your budget for food and other supplies. Ask yourself, is that excessive or not? If it is then reduce the budget allocated for that. If not, then adjust it accordingly minus any potential excesses that you have been making.

Again, we will go over all of these in greater detail when we get to chapter 4 of this book.

Step 5: Keep Your Spending Focused on Things That Last

As you go about repeating steps one to four mentioned earlier, you may notice that you will have some extra cash each month. Even though you are using a minimalist budget, you will still have to buy things and pay for things month after month.

However, each new month, you will have plenty of opportunities to decide and focus on things that last. For example, instead of buying dozens of bottled water each month, you can save up some money and just buy a high-quality water filter instead. This would allow you to save more money and help save the planet Earth in the process.

Each month you will notice that you may have spent too much money on paper towels. You can make the switch to cloth dish towels that you can wash, dry, and reuse. You may also notice that you keep on buying hand soap, dish detergent, and other cleaning products in small packages. You can later switch to larger packages which save you money and also help you go green.

The idea here is to learn how to focus on purchases that last longer than what you usually buy. Sure, it might seem like you're spending more, but remember that you are buying in bulk now. Whenever you buy in bulk, you always get a hefty discount so you end up saving more money in the end and in the long term.

Minimalism and Your Social Life

Oh, peer pressure is real. You will feel it more as you make adjustments in your lifestyle. Sometimes switching to a minimalist budget will make you ask whether it is worth it. You see, you might end up asking where the fun expenses will go.

Even if you use a minimalist budget, your friends and family will still be going to expensive gyms, getting over the budget spa treatments, buying over the top expensive coffee, and splurging in bars, restaurants, and shopping malls, and expensive boutiques.

Remember that using a minimalist budget is not supposed to be a painful experience. All you want to get is more control over your finances so you can have more money to achieve your financial goals like establishing a retirement fund, get a new and better car, start an investment or any other goal you may have determined that will be for your own benefit.

The good news is that a minimalist budget allows you to splurge from time to time. However, you will have to allocate a budget for it as well. It's what we will call a "fun fund" and we will go over the details of social life budgeting and other fun stuff in chapter 4 of this book. But just to give you an idea about it, remember that it is still your money and you will still have to decide how you can spend it.

You can't have much control over your budget if you're not allowed to use it to have fun, right? However, what you want to do is to put a spending limit on it as well. Is $500 for a night at the bar considered as a splurge but not too splurgy? That's up to you to decide.

What you want to do is to be able to maintain a social life but make sure that you remain kind to your good old wallet. You can even choose alternative activities with your friends instead of hitting the bar for the nth time this month.

Why not try some fun but budget-friendly options like:

- Weekend barbecues at your place
- Going on a picnic
- Walking on that trail that you guys have always talked about
- Binge-watching Netflix at home
- Go to free events in town where they serve free beer

Remember that the main goal of keeping to a minimalist budget is to have more control over your finances. It will be a lot more fun if you are able to have some fun with friends, being debt-free, and have a lot of extra cash at the end of

each month than spending your life away from
one paycheck to the next.

Key Takeaways

- Minimalist budgeting focuses on
  simplifying your finances

- It is not the most frugal budgeting system
  because it also emphasizes getting the
  best quality from things you actually
  spend on

- You start your journey into a minimalist
  budget with a change in your point of
  view

- Identify your financial priorities

- Switch to an ownership mindset

- Write down your financial goals

- Identify your MRCs and track your
  expenses

- Evaluate spending and categorize each
  expense that you have tracked

- Focus on expenses that last and things
  that are valuable

What You Can Do

Go back to the budget that you have tried. At this point, you should have at least tried any kind of budget for about a week. It's time to go through that budget.

Identify the following:

- What are your financial goals?

- Your income sources

- Write down all your expenses

- Categorize each expense into needs and wants

- Put all essential monthly recurring costs into a separate list

- Put all unessential expenses (including recurring ones like gym memberships, magazine subscriptions, video streaming, etc.) into a separate list

You will go through the details of your income sources, expenses, and goals in the next chapter and how you can fine-tune your budget even further. At this point, it's time to think long and hard about your financial goals and what

changes you need to make in order to achieve
them.

Chapter 3: Minimalist Budgeting Tips

In this chapter, we will go over the best minimalist living and budgeting tips that I have received as I transitioned into this philosophy and way of life. It was never an easy experience since I had to learn to let go of not just material possessions.

I also needed to learn to let go of old habits. I wasn't exactly a thrifty person and there is also that thing about being an impulsive buyer. In my journey toward practicing a minimalist budget, I had to learn to accept downsizing things.

I also had to make changes in my spending habits as well. But before we go deeper into my story, I would like to tell the story of a good friend of mine who also went through the same journey as I did.

That Serious Talk with Yourself and Accepting Harsh Realities

One of the first steps in the transition into a minimalist budget is to have that serious introspection and honestly reveal to yourself that you have truly messed things up big time financially.

I went through that and a good friend of mine by the name of Tess also had that serious talk with oneself as well. Here's here story:

> *Everything looked great the day when Tess was called in by her boss from Utah. They had those rare interviews that were more pleasant than others if you know what I mean.*
>
> *The occasion for this interview was for a job promotion. Tess worked for a garments and textile company as a quality assurance officer. Just like most employees there, she started all the way from the bottom—as a seamstress.*
>
> *On this day, her boss, with her distinct Utah accent, the two ladies had the most pleasant conversation. Tess was being promoted to a supervisor position for the QA Department.*

She was to replace the former QA chief who was retiring in the next couple of months. This promotion also meant a significant pay raise—about two tiers above her current pay grade.

Two months passed after this great news, Tess settled into her new role. She was great at it and her team loved how she treated everyone.

The pay was good, the work was good, but something changed in the next 12 months. With the pay raise came an increase in her spending habits. She bought new furniture, appliances, subscriptions, toys for her young boy Reuben, and a lot of other things.

They can afford these things now, so why not spend her hard-earned money on the things that they have always wanted, right?

In the next 12 months, her credit card bills ballooned over. It took a while for her to realize that she was, once again, living from paycheck to paycheck. The majority of the pay she received was spent paying for credit card debt.

It took about a year and a half for Tess to realize that her financial life was in jeopardy despite the huge amount of money she received month after month.

*We worked on these issues—Tess and I—
and we agreed upon a minimalist
budgeting strategy that was acceptable
to her. It was hard for her to accept the
reality she was living in.*

You see, you need to be honest about the status
of your finances first before you can make any
switch to any budgeting strategy—minimalist or
otherwise.

You need to learn new things but before you can
do that you need to accept who you currently are
and then let go. Bruce Lee, the martial arts
legend, once said:

*In order to taste my cup of water, you must
first empty your own cup. My friend, drop all of
your preconceived and fixed ideas and be
neutral. Do you know why this cup is useful?
Because it is empty.*

Once you have accepted the financial realities
that you are living with, it is easier to
understand why you have to change. If your
spending was without boundaries as it were,
then you will have to learn to set boundaries on
your expenses.

However, you first need to be honest with
yourself and admit that your current budgetary

strategy doesn't work. It's causing you stress. You need to understand that you need to learn to set boundaries on your expenses.

Without setting boundaries on your spending, then a minimalist budget (or any kind of budget for that matter) won't work.

Setting Financial Goals

The next tip is to set financial goals. You may have heard of SMART goals, right? It's quite popular nowadays. But if you're unfamiliar with it, here's what it is in a nutshell. It's actually a mnemonic or an acronym, which stands for:

- S – specific
- M – measurable
- A – actionable
- R – relevant
- T – time-bound.

According to this theory, the goals you set should be specific enough. Let's say instead of making it your goal to be rich, you should identify a specific criterion that can help you identify as someone who is rich.

An example of that is having a million dollars in the bank. That's a specific goal, right? Since it is specific, a million dollars is definitely measurable. You can determine how much money you need to save in order to reach that goal.

It should be actionable—that means your goals shouldn't be vague—they should be things that you can act upon. They should also be relevant to you. You don't want to set being an Olympic swimmer as one of your goals if you're not really interested in swimming anyway.

Finally, your goals also need to be time-bound. That means you should set a deadline when you really have to achieve your stated goal. Using our current example, you will determine or estimate how long would it take for you to save up to a million dollars in your bank account?

Let's say, you can save up to $100,000 each month (hypothetically speaking). Let's say you can save up to $41,700 each month—or something around that figure. In a year's time, you would have saved $500,400. If you can continue saving that amount for two years, then you would have saved up to $1,000,800 and you would have reached your goal.

So, your goal, to be truly SMART, you need to save $41,700 each month and to do that for a total of 24 months.

Making Your SMART Goals Minimalistic

Now, if the math we mentioned earlier is starting a slight headache, then here's a simple way that you can do it. Forget the 1 million dollars. Forget the 24 months or two years because keeping track of your financial records for a period of 2 years can be a bit too hard for some.

What you can do is to be specific and measure things in the short-term. How do you minimalize your goals? Here's one way you can do it:

1. Choose a goal—a small goal that you can reach either each week or each month.
2. Determine if it is something that you can realistically achieve—maybe $41,000 is way too much for your finances can currently handle.
3. Finally, set your deadline to 30 days.

Here's an example. Instead of focusing on a million dollars in 24 months, you can make it your goal to save $1,000 each month or after 30 days.

That's it.

Now, break that down for each day—then you can divide a thousand bucks by 30, and you end up with $33 a day as your daily quota. You can then set up a piggy bank and just drop 33 dollars each day.

After making that $33 daily goal, forget about the $1,000. Stick to that $33 and mark off each day on your calendar when you are able to set aside $33. The goal is to mark off all the days on your calendar.

This is a pressure-free and simpler goal-setting strategy.

Distancing Yourself from Financial Distractions

Financial distractions are everywhere. You can find them on TV, the mall, the grocery store, in your email, and even in the apps you use on your phone. They come in a variety of forms such as notifications, commercials, mail orders, email offer subscriptions, social media posts, online streaming video, and many more.

The marketing strategies that sales folks use nowadays are meant to grab and trap your attention. The ultimate goal is to convince you to spend your money on the things that they are selling, whether you need it or not.

Of course, this whimsical and spur of the moment spending decisions is against minimalist philosophy and practice.

So, how do you avoid financial distractions? Here are a few tips:

Get Out of the Comparison Game

Stop comparing yourself to other people—that's a hard and fast rule right there. Someone once said that if you play the comparison game, you end up in a financial death trap.

Your life is your own and each person goes through a different set of circumstances. Some may look successful, but they never went through the same kinds of hardships and stresses that you went through. They may have had it easy and maybe they may have had it worse.

Your life is your life and your values are your values—a friend of mine once quoted, I still don't know who said that originally. Don't get excited over what society tells you are important. If it doesn't align with your values—i.e. minimalist values, then you have no business getting mixed up in it.

All these so-called "important" things that become popular today, and then gone tomorrow, are actually nothing more than financial distractions. They wear you down and break your momentum.

Here's a fact—it takes time and a lot of effort to actually grow wealth. You have no time for distractions. So how do you know if something that has caught your attention something worth investing in? You can use the first minimalist acid test below.

The Minimalist Acid Test #1

Here's an acid test, as it were, that you can use before you spend money or invest money on anything. When that happens, ask yourself the following questions:

- Will this expense align with my minimalist goals?
- Can I purchase this without incurring any debt?
- Do I really need to buy this now?
- Can I spend money on this thing and still be a minimalist?
- Is this item of good quality and will it last many years?

If you can answer all five questions with a big YES, then by all means use your money on that item or investment. If not, then don't spend your money and forget whatever it is and move on.

Define Your Core Minimalist Values

We mentioned earlier that minimalist thinking and philosophy focus on living more with less. It also involves focusing on quality items and an emphasis on building life experiences.

Those are great minimalist core values, but they're not the only ones. There are many more. The thing is you need to define your own core minimalist values. No one can dictate that for you.

Some people may add some religious values in the mix, and still, others may also incorporate leadership principles as well. It's all up to you. Here are a few minimalist values that you may want to consider adding to your own core values as a human being.

- Getting life achievements
- A sense of adventure
- Earning authenticity
- Being an established authority in your respective field of expertise
- Gain autonomy and independence
- Establish work-life balance
- Beauty
- Practice boldness without being overbearing
- Accept and take on challenges

68

- Practice compassion
- Patriotism and citizenship
- Sense of community
- Establish creativity
- Be curious, not judgmental
- Determination
- Always practice fairness
- Faith
- Become famous
- Honesty
- Find happiness
- Be an influencer
- Leadership
- Love for mankind
- Keeping kindness
- Seek for learning
- Practice openness
- Meaningful work
- Optimism first
- Seek pleasure
- Religion, spirituality, and other religious values
- Always practice respect
- Establish the security of the family
- Service
- Seek success
- Self-respect

- Work for wisdom
- Become a wealth builder

Note that there can be more personal values that you can include in your own list of core values. What is important at this point is for you to identify all the things that you value. Make a list of at least 10 core values—include the primary minimalist values of living with less, focusing on quality, and seeking out enriching personal experiences.

Key Takeaways

- Identify how much you are really making each month

- After identifying how much you take home each month, know whether you are living below your means or not. Honestly evaluate whether you are spending more than you make or not.

- Be specific about your financial goals

- How do you measure your success?

- Identify what you need to do in order to achieve those goals

- When do you want to achieve them?

- Identify the long term but for now, focus on the short-term: a 30-day plan.

- Minimize financial distractions

- Identify your core and minimalist values—what are the things that you really care about

- Reflect on those values each day

What You Can Do

You need to go through that same harrowing self-talk that Tess went through especially if you're really living above your means (i.e. you're spending more than what you earn).

A really important thing that you can do right now is to identify and draw your attention to your core values. After you identify the things that really matter to you, you can better decide on what to do with the expenditures that you are making.

Identify your financial distractions and get rid of them. For instance, if you have four credit cards (the average nowadays) then cancel three and just live with one. If you can live without any, then do so.

The goal at this point is to become more aware of your financial situation and become more mindful of how you spend your money. We will also go over strategies on how to reduce your expenses.

Chapter 4: The Secret Financial Formula for Minimalist Budgeting Success

In the previous chapters, we have covered topics like what is a minimalist budget, its functions, and sample minimalist budgets so you can try it out right away, how to start a minimalist budget, focusing on quality over quantity, and controlling emotional spending among other things.

Meet Javvy

In this chapter we will go through some of the minimalist budgeting principles as they were taught to me by my mentor—we'll call him Javvy, well, his real name is Javier. He made his first million dollars at age 26.

We first met when my family moved to his town around 8 years ago. I was having problems with my computer equipment and I couldn't find the parts I needed. I needed it for my home-based work. I also had a pending deadline so I got desperate.

I worked on that computer for about three days. I even had a technician come over to verify my findings. And yes, I needed a new RAM stick or DIMM (dual inline memory module).

Unfortunately, no one had the particular one I needed. They offered me something with less RAM but that just won't work for me. It would make my computer's performance too slow and I wouldn't get the job done in time that way.

After three days of testing and searching, I was about to give up. My wife invited me to a gathering or activity in church so I went. I felt downtrodden and I knew I wasn't going to get the job done in time—that meant penalties on the deal I made, i.e. I'll get less money for the work I was doing.

That afternoon while at the children's activity, I met Javvy. He was standing at the doorway greeting everyone who came in. I was a new face in town so he approached me and we talked.

You can call it fate or whatever, but at the time he needed a web monkey to manage his websites—back then he was doing affiliate marketing (this was in the pre-Penguin and all those Google animal updates).

On top of that, he had an extra computer that he could loan to me while waiting for the part I ordered. In an instant, I had a new client and a computer that I could use to finish the current project I was working on.

And that was how we met.

When we first met he was just on the verge of earning his first million. Back then he was doing affiliate marketing, merchandising, and logistics. He partnered with his brother-in-law with the logistics business.

Nowadays he has created around seven income streams (I think). What captivated me about him was that he was 10 years younger than me, smart, and adventurous. You can say that I was humble enough to accept the fact that this younger fella was doing far better than me.

I consider him one of my mentors despite his age. What I present here are his minimalistic budgeting strategy and principles. At times he would describe it as the budgeting and financial formula used by millionaires.

How to Stick with a Minimalist Budget

Chances are, even after you have tried all the tips and advice that we have covered in the previous chapter, and even after a month of trying out minimalist budgeting, it is quite possible that your expenses are equal to or even greater than your current income.

If that is the case (don't worry, that was my problem too even with direct tutelage from Javvy), there are two options available to you:

1. Find ways to slash cut back on your expenses
2. Find ways to earn extra income

This entire process will be difficult and at times it can be very discouraging, especially if you go over your budget one time or the other. Remember that you're not the first one to experience how difficult it is to implement a budget.

However, do take note that those who persist, remain patient, and remain resilient despite their failures, are the ones who have achieved long-term success. Consider the following principles and tips.

Reducing Your Expenses

Reducing your expenses is at the heart of minimalist budgeting. If you're looking for budgeting strategies, it is highly probable that you are spending more than you earn. One obvious side effect of spending more than your means is that you live from paycheck to paycheck each month and that you often use your credit card to cover for part of your monthly expenses.

Do you sometimes feel like you never get ahead? Well, part of that feeling comes from the fact that what you earn each month is not enough ergo the second part of this strategy (i.e. find ways to increase your income) which we will go over later in this chapter.

There are a few minimalist principles when it comes to cutting down on your spending. Remember that what you're looking for in minimalist budgeting is to increase quality and not quantity. The main idea is to limit and eventually omit the things that you don't really need and seek for quality in your life and in the things that you possess.

Here are a few things you should keep in mind:

- Look around your home and in your place of work. Find things that you really need and identify the things that you don't actually need. Keep buying the things that you need and stop buying things that you don't need. If your finances need an overhaul, focus your spending on your needs.
- You waste money and time if you get rid of unnecessary items now but then end up buying more unnecessary things later.

For instance, you may have resolved to sell your used clothing. But then you end up buying more clothes that you don't really need anyway. Plug the holes in your budget; stop buying the things that you don't need.

- Check your fridge. What sort of food do you store? Do you eat that kind of food? Here's a rule of thumb to live by: store what you always eat and eat whatever you store. You may have heard that eating cabbages can help you lose weight. You buy a week's worth of cabbages, but you end up not even eating half of them. That is a waste. Buy and store only the food that you eat.

- What activities do you spend money on? Do you really need to pay for that gym membership? Do you really need to subscribe to that fashion magazine? Do you really need that exclusive pass to the city's concert hall? Spend money on activities that enrich you and those that you truly value. Did you sign up for the gym because your friends asked you to? If you didn't really want to do in the first place then there's no point in keeping that gym membership.

- Check your hobbies. How many hobbies do you have? Do you really need that new pair of Nikes? Will that new pair of basketball shoes allow you to enjoy basketball better or are you just buying it to show off? Do you really need that new graphics card for your digital art or are you just want to get the latest gear?

Evaluate how you spend your money on food, your hobbies, your activities, the food you eat, and the things you buy at home and at work.

Note that the expense of reducing tips that you will see below will be based on the minimalist principles that we have mentioned. Here are the tips:

Top Expense Reducing Tips

The following are some expense slashing tips that I have learned over time. They come from a variety of sources. Some were taught to me by friends, some were used by colleagues who were really great at money management, and others came through trial and error.

1. ***Sell that car you don't really need***. If not the car then maybe that other

vehicle you have in the garage that is just taking up space. This came as a wake-up call to me when I was evaluating my expenses. It was a big lesson learned.

2. ***Use public transport*** if it saves you time and money.

3. You can just **carpool to work** to save money on gas and fare.

4. ***Keep your car's tires inflated properly***. Every 2 PSI you get on your tires improves your car's mileage by one percent—it also saves you gas since your car's engine won't have to work so hard.

5. If you always pay your credit card bill on time every month you can request a ***rate reduction***, which helps you save money.

6. **Use automatic debt repayments**. This will ensure that you have money allotted to your debts and that you don't unwittingly spend that money on something else that you don't really need.

7. Open a separate bank account for your emergency fund so you don't spend it.

Remember this one rule: every amount of cash you withdraw from the bank will tend to get spent one way or another. So, keep your emergency fund in a separate account—**AND** automate the debits to that account from your main account.

8. ***Consolidate your debts at 0% APR***. We will go over debt reduction strategies in chapter 7 of this book. Apart from that we also cover debts in book 2 of this series. For now, just remember that if you can find a balance transfer that offers 0% APR and that will last to at least 18 months then that might be a good deal.

   However, there is **<u>one caveat</u>**—make sure that you can pay the entire debt amount in that 18 month period. That may allow you to save a bit of money on the interest and you can take advantage of the 0% APR offer.

   If you can't make all the payments (do the math) within 18 months, then this might not be the best strategy for you. This debt reduction strategy is only applicable to a few who can afford to consolidate their debts.

9. ***Move to a less expensive part of
   town***. The cost of living in one area may
   be lower than in others. If that is the case
   you should move there especially if it can
   significantly reduce your expenses for a
   while.

   Some people overlook this option when
   they're finding ways to reduce their
   expenses. You don't have to move
   overseas or become an ex-pat. You can
   move to other areas in your town or city
   that may have lower rent and cost of
   living. Maybe you can move to a different
   city, town, or state.

   Before you move, check if you can find
   employment there. It would be better if
   you can get signed up for a job prior to
   your move. If not, at least find out how
   much is the average salary in that area so
   you can estimate your potential monthly
   budget.

   Check the housing costs too—this should
   be a big factor. In many instances, if you
   live in the city or in any highly urbanized
   area, you can significantly reduce your

cost of living by simply moving to suburban or rural areas.

10. ***Eliminate any consumable habits***. We have talked about this earlier. Some habits require money—and in some instances, a huge chunk of money. Examples of such habits are excessive drinking and smoking. As we have pointed out, sometimes you won't notice them eating up your budget then you have a choice.

You can choose to keep them as your habits or you can quit. You decide. However, if you don't want to cut ties with the bottle or the cigarette stick, you can choose to reduce your consumption instead.

However, if you are serious about it, you should get help to overcome your dependence on such substances. You will not only give your wallet a big bump, but you will also turn things around in terms of your health.

11. ***Reduce salon and grooming time***. We have mentioned this before and we're

just going to elaborate on it a little bit. Notice how often you cut and style your hair. How often do you go to the salon? Do you go to manicure parties with your friends?

You should also check out how much you spend on shampoos, eye creams, and other beauty products. Instead of buying high end and really expensive products, try to find more affordable options that also offer the same kind of experience. You don't need to spend a truckload of money just to look pretty.

12. ***Stop spending too much money on clothes***. This is something I learned from my Korean friends Lijun and Mr. Kim. We met in a winter English camp where kids from Korea come over during the winter to learn English directly from native speakers.

We went out shopping one time and all they bought were just a magazine and some snacks. On my part, I bought five shirts. They told me I was spending a lot of money on clothing.

I told them that it was my thing. They told me I was wasting money. I later noticed that both of them only brought a handful of clothes for the trip—they love to pack light. But they never bothered to buy new shirts or pants or anything.

They were satisfied with the few clothes that they had. I later learned how much money I was wasting on signature shirts and NBA jerseys. I ended up selling them in a garage sale and I was able to make money off of them.

13. *Learn to DIY*: do you hire others to do a lot of the chores in the house? If you're short on cash, why not do everything yourself? You can mow the lawn, fix the leak in the sink, and repair your own car. If it saves you money to DIY then go for it.

14. *Focus on one sport at a time*. If you or your children love sports, you should only focus on only one sport at a time. The real cost behind each of these sporting activities is in the gear that you buy. If you or your kids sign up for jiu-jitsu, notice that you spend a lot of money

on the gi, mats, and other gear and outfits. What if you switch to another sport, say archery? You spend money again on the equipment for that sport. Focusing on one sport at a time will give your wallet a break, enough for your finances to recover.

15. **_Reduce childcare costs_**. Note that at times there will be more affordable childcare options. You can also cut back on child care needs at least for one day or maybe two. You can work at a later shift once a week so you can stay home to take care of the kids until your spouse gets home.

16. **_Switch to a more affordable cellphone plan_**. Do you need that $90 Verizon unlimited data plan or can you settle for the $35 prepaid plan? If the latter works for you and you are still able to do the things you need to do with your phone, then quit the former and switch to the more affordable plan. Changing to the latter can save you $660 a year.

If you don't really need that much data per month or you can do without the other features, then downgrading your plan is a smart decision.

17. ***Get term life insurance instead***. Check your policy and see if you're paying for term life insurance or universal/whole life insurance. Note that term life insurance is cheaper and it is significantly more affordable than whole life insurance. Yes, term life is a lot easier on your budget even if you're getting the same type of coverage.

    But what's the difference? The difference is that your policy in term insurance will terminate usually by the time you retire. It is presumed that your family is no longer dependent on your income when you retire.

    On the other hand, the policies for whole life insurance cover you for your entire lifetime. It is a lot more expensive though. Consider getting term insurance if you're a bit tight on the budget.

18. ***Auto and homeowners insurance***. If you still have strong credit, you may want to shop around either auto insurance or

homeowner's insurance. Ask for quotes from different providers and see if you can get substantial savings if you do make the switch.

However, if you do find a provider that can provide you a really good offer, tell your current provider about it. Give them a chance to match it. If they can come up with an offer that is as good or almost as good as the other party, then take their new offer and stay with them.

Here's another thing that might be helpful to you—ask if your provider (or another provider) can bundle the two policies together. Most insurance companies can accommodate that request and you tend to save a good amount of money when you bundle the two policies together.

19. ***Buy the store brand or generic goods***. Buying generic or store brand products may help you save a good deal of money especially if you shop for groceries at the same store every time.

Check the ingredients of the different goods you buy and then compare that to the brand name products that you usually purchase. If the ingredients have the same ingredients you can try it once to see if it is just as good.

Even if they're nearly the same, you can just try it once and then you can decide if you want to switch to the generic instead of the brand name product.

20. ***Grow your own food***. Growing your own food at home is more than just a hobby. It's actually a worthy vocation—not to mention something that can potentially relieve people of so much stress.

If you do it right, with some practice, you can even raise vegetables in your own yard (or indoors if you have space) to turn a profit. Focus on growing vegetables that you eat. It is pointless growing broccoli if you don't really like the taste of that vegetable, right?

21. ***Buy in bulk***. This is conventional wisdom —you get savings every time you

buy in bulk. This is a really good idea in case you're shopping for non-perishable goods like detergents, shampoos, cleaners, bath soaps, etc. You can also buy food items in bulk especially if these items have a long shelf life.

22. *Use coupons and coupon codes*. Sometimes coupons let you save a significant amount on everyday items— well, some don't so you better check how much of a discount you can get with each coupon or coupon code that you can find.

 Now, in case a coupon/code does give you significant savings, combine that with our previous tip—buy the applicable item or items in bulk so you can get more savings.

23. **Limit dining out or taking take-out meals**. Fine dining, dining out, and buying take-out dinners represent a huge luxury. The amount of money you spend on these food orders tend to increase when you buy them for your entire family.

Reduce the number of times you go out for a meal and opt for more home-cooked meals. Consider doing some meal planning so you can have your meals prepared ahead of time.

Don't choose really elaborate recipes. When it comes to home-cooked meals, sometimes the simplest dishes taste the best. Use fresh ingredients so you get the most flavors from the food that you cook. Remember that cooking is a life skill that can go a long way.

24. **Reduce the number of paid services**: look at how many services you are subscribed to each month. You can even include services by a gardener, Netflix, and other streaming services, gym memberships (coz you're basically paying for the gym coach's service), tutorial and online training activities, the nanny, and others.

Find out which of these services you can reduce. For instance, you can go to the gym twice a month instead of going there twice each week. Instead of paying for the monthly fee, you can go on a per session fee. Here's another option—set up your home gym instead so you don't have to pay for any gym fees ever. You can just consult with the coach directly from time to time depending on the level of your training.

Check how many video streaming services you subscribe to. Do you also have cable? Doesn't that seem redundant? You already have cable and you're still streaming stuff on Netflix. Can't you just pick one or the other? Hint: choose the video service that you watch more often. Here's a potential alternative—quit all video services and just watch regular TV. If you want really good stories, then go read a book instead since a lot of the really good movies are based on novels.

Tip: look for ways to do certain things yourself like looking after the kids more often rather than hiring a nanny or mowing the lawn yourself instead of hiring a gardener. When you're having financial problems you can stop hiring for now. You need to put a plug on all avenues where cash is flowing out so you can have every dollar that you can use.

25. **Are you still subscribed to newspapers or magazines**? Cancel them and just read their content online—everyone's switching to online platforms anyway.

26. **Reduce travel expenses**. How often do you have those weekend getaways? How often do you take your kids to their grandparents' place? Look into your travel expenses and see if you can reduce your travel expenses by visiting or traveling less often. Consider using technology in case your kids want to see your relatives—try Zoom or other video conferencing software so you can stay in touch.

27. **Consider volunteering**: volunteering to work in soup kitchens or other charitable causes reduces the focus on you yourself. This helps you think less about your needs and consider the needs of others. Who knows, it may even help you want to buy unnecessary things and give you a paradigm shift. Some people

have learned to content and genuinely happy with the stuff they already own simply because they realized through humanitarian service how fortunate they truly are compared to many people in the world.

28. **Do a cash-only month.** Are you haunted by a repeating cycle of credit card debt that goes away and comes back the next month? It may mean that you are using your credit card way too much and it is eating away at your monthly budget. Consider going for an entire month using only actual cash when paying for everything. Grab your credit cards and put them in a box and hide them in the closet where you can easily forget about them. One month—just one month and see the benefits of not seeing extra lines in your credit card bill.

29. **Use the one-in-one-out rule.** The one-in-one-out rule goes like this: before you buy something (a new pair of running shoes for example), consider the running shoes you already have. Is it still good? If it is then don't buy the new pair that you saw on sale earlier. If you do buy the new

pair, make sure that you sell or give away the old pair of running shoes. That way you reduce the clutter at home and you have created a way to control certain expenses.

30. **Are you still paying for a lot of club memberships**? If you have plenty of club memberships that have monthly or annual subscriptions and fees, then consider reducing the number of these memberships. If you really need to stay within social circles, choose one or two that you frequently attend and must be at. If you don't have many friends in the golf club and you don't really want to play golf anyway, then cancel your golf club membership.

31. **Do some air sealing**. It might not seem obvious but air sealing your home will help you save money especially if you're living in an old house. A lot of these older homes experience a constant draft. The loss of warm air during the winter (or cool air during summer) can cost you. Air sealing ensures that you keep your house warm/cold and thus saves you some

money that you would have otherwise
spent on extra utility bills.

32. **Use a lower temperature setting for
your hot water**. Another way that you
can save is by lowering the temperature
of your hot water heater. Drop it down to
125 to 130 degrees.

33. **Unplug any electrical appliance that
you're not using**. This prevents any
phantom charges on your bill. Remember
that they still consume a bit of electricity
and the more appliances and gadgets you
leave plugged in will add up to your next
bill. You can also use power strips and
timers to automatically turn off the
charge to anything that's plugged into the
outlets. Use smart power strips to make
the system more efficient.

34. **Install programmable thermostat**.
Programmable thermostats can
automatically adjust your home's
temperature settings as needed. This can
help make significant savings from
month to month.

35. **Switch to LED bulbs**. Are you still using those old light bulbs? Switching to LEDs will also help save you money.

Javvy's Simple Formula to Increase Savings

Why do you have to go through the trouble of finding ways to save money? The reason behind that is actually very simple. You can't get ahead in your finances, even if you're using a minimalist budget if you're still spending like you have an infinite sum of money.

You can track all your expenses as much as you want but if you don't do something to stop those cash flow leaks from going out of your pocket, then your minimalist budget just won't work.

Here's a simple formula that my good friend taught me:

Expense = Income - Financial Fund

What does that mean? Here's what it means. When you get your paycheck, the first thing you need to do is to automatically put away money to a certain financial fund or funds if you want to. This financial fund can be anything from your life savings, emergency fund, play fund (we'll get to that in a minute), or investment fund.

Since this chapter is all about making savings, let's do that first. Every time you get your paycheck you immediately take away a designated percentage of that money and put it in a savings account. Use a separate bank account if possible – if not then just use an envelope that you can keep inside your home and away from your own reach.

The leftover amount after you have taken away your savings is the money that you will use for your expenses. Use this frame of mind each time you do that:

"Consider your savings as an expense— something that you are obligated to pay."

Make it a habit.

Make it a habit to pay yourself first by spending money on your savings first before other expenses. Doing this immediately and if possible automatically each time you get your pay for your work will make it a habit.

Habitually saving money will be your key to better managing your finances. It doesn't matter how much you put into your savings account. What matters is that you establish the habit of saving.

As financial author T. Harv Eker once said—*the habit is more important than the amount.*

And finally, one way to ensure that you have enough money after you have put away money towards your savings fund is to cut down on your expenses.

People usually use this alternative formula when it comes to their finances:

Savings = Income - Expense

What this means is that you spend whatever it is you need to spend first, and then whatever is left, if any, will be used for your savings.

Remember that the formula above is the antithesis of the savings formula that we just mentioned earlier. This is the usual formula that a lot of people use which is why they don't have any money left for savings or investments at all.

Now apart from a savings account, we have mentioned that there are several other financial funds that you should have. But before we discuss these other funds, let's answer a very fundamental question that a lot of people ask about their savings:

"How much of savings should I have?"

The answer to that is that amount of your savings is up to you but you need to create a goal. Your savings should be a different account from your emergency fund and other stashes of cash.

We'll go over more about those funds and cash stashes later in this chapter.

Just remember that your savings can be a mini-savings amount. You don't have to aim for a million dollars just yet. But let's say that you have a lot of debt and you can only afford to put away $100 into that savings fund. Then start with that. But that shouldn't be your only savings goal. Your long-term savings goal should be a lot more substantial.

I would like to suggest that if you don't have any savings at all then make it a goal to save $1,000 in 10 months. You can do that by putting away $100 each time you receive your pay until you save up to a thousand dollars.

A thousand dollars might sound meager for some. But if you really don't have anything left in your bank account at the end of each month, then having that much money in-store when your next paycheck arrives is a significant improvement from zero.

Once you have that much saved, move on to saving a different fund. You can open another account if you want. This time, you will also put away $100 or more for your next financial fund. What funds are these? Here they are:

- The emergency fund/lifeline fund
- The charity fund/tithing fund

- The continuing education fund/self-investment fund
- The fun fund
- The financial freedom fund
- The expense fund

Let's go over each of these financial funds in detail.

Emergency Fund/Lifeline Fund

In life, you should expect the unexpected. We often say that emergencies are things that we don't expect. You don't see it coming, which is why you call it an emergency. But what if you have already expected an emergency to come along and have prepared for it no matter what it is? Will you be more at ease and more composed and a lot less panicky about it?

The answer is YES, right?

Expect emergencies and prepare for them by creating an emergency fund. This is the next fund that you should save up for after you have created your savings fund. Sometimes having an emergency fund spells the difference between scrambling for funds and being at peace despite the financial storm that's already there pouring down on you.

Your emergency fund will come in handy during tough times such as:

- Unemployment
- Huge car fixes
- Appliance repair or replacement
- Major repairs to your home
- Unforeseen medical expenses

The Financial Emergency Acid Test

The items in the list above are actual financial emergencies. How can you tell if it is a real emergency or not? If a situation or expense is absolutely essential or unavoidable and it has a significant impact on your cash flow, then consider it as a financial emergency.

For instance, when an appliance or tool you use for gaining income breaks down, then that is a financial emergency. Let's say you bake cakes for a living and your oven breaks down, then that is a real emergency.

You can't bake so you can't earn money and it disrupts your capability to earn.

On the other hand, getting a replacement oven when you don't use it to make money is not an essential expense and thus does not constitute a financial emergency. The same goes for that big sale for that new pair of Nikes.

How Big Should Be Your Emergency Fund?

So, how much of an emergency fund should you save? The ideal answer to that is anywhere from 6 months to 1-year's worth of your expenses. So, if you spend $2,000 each month on everything (needs + wants) then you will need an emergency fund of at least $12,000. We already talked about this in Chapter 1 of this book, remember?

But, what if things aren't going well for you? The long answer is that everything will have to depend on your personal circumstances. I mentioned earlier in the previous chapter that you should set aside at least 10% of your pay each month as funds for emergencies.

However, what if you are already having problems making ends meet? That is where all the methods of saving money that we talked about earlier come in. Find ways to save money and save what you can towards your emergency fund.

Treat it like there is an emergency already about to happen. If you don't have an emergency fund right now, then treat it like it's a life or death situation. You must make some kind of emergency fund in the next few months (or weeks if necessary).

The Starter Emergency Fund Amount! – So what if you're really out of luck and you can't save enough money whatever you do. 10% saved towards your emergency fund each month and/or say $6,000 is a long shot for you given your current financial situation. It might even take you a year to save that amount, so what now?

The answer: reduce your EF (emergency fund) goal. Reduce your EF goal to $1,000 (yeah, just like what we did with the savings fund) and then try to save as much each month. Let's say after all your efforts at being thrifty and minimalistic only allow you to save $200 each month. Well then that's okay. It's better to have $200 for an emergency than having nothing at all.

Here's an important point: never use your savings for emergencies as much as possible. Your savings is for your future, and you don't want to use what you have in store for the future to fix the mistakes of the past.

However, in the next five months, if you stay consistent with it, you can save

$1,000 for your emergency fund. Better than nothing, right?

Make this $1,000 a priority. Once you have saved up at least $1,000 and you're still able to keep things afloat financially then move on to the next fund described below. Never ever use that EF for anything except for an emergency (i.e. unemployment, medical bills, home, and car repair).

The next question is where do you put the money? If your EF is only a small amount, let's say $1,000 to $5,000 then just keep it in the bank or at home. The important thing about this fund is that it should be accessible to you just in case an emergency does happen.

Don't put it in an investment or even in a time deposit. You won't be able to withdraw those funds for immediate use. You can invest it in a financial instrument provided that it is liquid enough—meaning you can get the funds ASAP maybe within a day or two or at most the next 72 hours.

You don't want to be cash-less within a 24 to 72 hour period. Having no cash for more than 3 days is already quite ridiculous.

Expense Fund

We already talked about identifying monthly recurring costs (MRCs) in a previous chapter. That means you should already have an idea just how much money you're going to have to spend on bills, food, groceries, rent, and other MRCs.

BIG QUESTION: With that in mind, how do you know if you're financially afloat or if your finances are about to sink simply because you can't keep up with your monthly recurring costs?

The Expense (MRC) Acid Test: here's one of Javvy's secrets—it's a rule of thumb actually. Here it is: if you can keep your MRC to about 50% of your monthly income (from all sources), then you are financially afloat. Keep it that way for at least 12 months and you will eventually have enough money for savings, emergencies, investments, and others.

But what if you have tried everything to be frugal? You can't reduce your expenses any further. What now?

The solution is to find other sources of income. Warren Buffet once said that people shouldn't depend on only one income. Depending on only one income stream is a recipe for disaster.

Do you know that the average millionaire has around 7 income streams? If you want to be financially free, then you need more income sources.

106

Yes, these well to do people have jobs and they may even have a side job too. But they don't depend on these jobs. Some may even do their jobs for free or for a very small salary. Would you believe that? But they have other income streams as well. They also have passive income sources too.

If your current income only goes to MRCs then you're in deep trouble. You should look for other sources of income. We'll cover that in a little while after we've covered all the funds.

So, as a review, your acid test to figure out if you're financially afloat is that if your MRCs only reach up to 50% of your monthly budget/income. If it goes over, then you need to find another source of income so you won't be left cash strapped each month. If you can find ways to reduce your MRCs to less than 50% then you're doing a lot better.

Note that the $2,000 amount for MRCs (mentioned above) is only an example. According to the latest available figures released by the US Bureau of Labor and Statistics, the average monthly expenditure for households in the US is around $5,000.

This is based on 2017 data, which is the most recently available data at the time of this writing. They may have 2018 and 2019 data ready but they haven't made it public just yet as I write this book. Perhaps they just can't get it done given the current pandemic that we're all facing nowadays.

The Fun Fund

Some people call this the play fund or some other name but of course they're referring to the self-same thing. This is the amount of money you put away for your leisure. This is the money you use so that you can have fun ergo its name.

As the saying goes, "All work and no play makes Jack a dull boy."

You deserve to enjoy the fruits of your labors, right? That's another saying. If you're not having fun, then work and all the other things you're doing won't be as much fun either. One of the purposes of working hard is to give you time to enjoy life.

That is why you need to set aside some money for your enjoyment.

The good news is that you get to decide how much you put into this fun fund. Just remember that this is your spending limit for any leisure activities like going to the bar, road tripping, money for the gym, party money, weekend getaways, etc.

You can even save your fun fund and defer any non-essential activities for several months so that you can accumulate enough of a fun fund to really go somewhere and splurge.

Your fun fund is the money that will keep you sane. I know the feeling of working all day, day in and day out, seven days a week, 30 days a month. After a week of solid work, you just go nuts.

You need a way to lose some steam. And to do that will cost you money—a lot of times. But there are ways to take the edge off without spending too much. So, how big the fun fund will be is all up to you.

Self-Investment Fund

This is one of the things that a lot of people have neglected. After college, people think that they're done with studying and they don't want to pick up another book in their life. But that's not the right attitude if you really want to succeed in life.

Personal development, New York Times best-selling author, and speed reading coach Jim Kwik once said that leaders are readers. He pointed out that the average CEO reads 4 or 5 books a month. Warren Buffet, business tycoon and philanthropist, is said to read 500 pages each day, devoting a huge amount of his time to reading.

Some of the most successful people take the time to attend seminars, participate in master classes, attend online training, and watch instructional videos. Learning should be an ongoing process for everyone.

Here's an important note that I learned from Javvy:

"Prosperity comes with personal growth. You can't expect to have a more financially secure life without changing and growing for the better. If you want to bless your life and the lives of the people you love, then you must strive to become a better version of yourself.

"Financial growth and personal growth go hand in hand."

You don't have to spend a lot of money on training and you don't need to travel to seminars either. Today is the day of online courses, webinars, and free online training. Zoom is the latest buzzword.

Let's say you find training from Mind Valley or from Jim Kwik's Kwik Learning or any other coach online. There are lots of them nowadays.

110

You can try the free masterclasses or webinars first and if you think that you like what they're providing then you can sign up for their online courses. Some webinars may cost you a couple of hundred dollars or more. However, on average, it would cost you a little over $100 for a 1-hour coaching session or web-based training.

You can set aside a little amount of money for the paid training and attend the free ones for now. When you have enough money for the paid version, then spend that money on that training. This is an investment in yourself. The more you read, train, and practice what you have learned, the better a person you will become.

The Charity Fund/Tithing Fund

The first time Javvy told me that he was giving 10% of his annual income to the church I thought he was crazy. Well, he was rich so eventually, I figured that he did it simply because he could afford it.

But then one day he told me that he even paid that tithe even when his sales were low. He paid it consistently even if business wasn't that good.

I'm not a completely religious person—I like my happy hours and such—but my mentor taught me that giving to charity or tithes to your church does something to your brain. It changes your point of view.

Giving away your hard-earned money without expecting anything in return gives you a paradigm shift. In his words, he says that it "rewires your mind."

How does giving that money away rewire your brain?

It's based on actual science (big grin!)

Here are the reasons:

1. According to studies published in Nature Communications, a scholarly journal, when you behave generously, it <u>neurologically wires your mind towards happiness</u>. In short, you become happier when you are genuinely generous.

2. That means generosity creates a paradigm shift—a prosperity mindset. Suddenly, you don't feel like you're in need because you realize that you have the power to help others.

3. Generosity tends to be reciprocated in general. When a community is generous, it makes the entire community a safer place to be. People become kinder and

better to live with. According to one study
published in the Journal of Personality
and Social Psychology, when people
experience generous giving from others,
<u>they tend to become more generous</u>
themselves.

4. When you give back to others and when
    they give back to you without expecting
    any reward in return, it creates
    interpersonal trust. It also increases
    social engagement thus you are able to
    find more financial opportunities. You
    network with key players even better
    when you are generous—people can sense
    that. According to a study published by
    Stanford University, communities with
    better social engagements like these tend
    to have people who live longer lives.

5. Giving away to charitable causes equals a
    tax write-off. If you make sure to process
    your donation via a registered 501(c)(3)
    organization then you can expect a <u>tax
    refund</u>.

The Financial Freedom Fund

Yeah, the Financial Freedom Fund is an organization that gives grants to students but that's not what I'm referring to. This fund is what you will use for making investments. So, let's call it an investment fund as well. This is one of the last funds you're going to make and you should be building it gradually.

Here's a tip: you can't build your financial freedom fund or investment fund if you're still in debt. You can't make a sizable investment in anything if you are hounded by collectors. Pay your debts as fast as you can. The sooner you get out of debt the faster you'll be able to create investments. One of the best ways to do that is to follow a minimalist budget which basically de-clutters your finances.

I also asked that question myself—in case I get a bonus from my current job, will it be better to put that money in an investment or use it to pay for my debts? The answer is simple. If the return on that investment is thrice the amount of the interest you have to pay on your debt and that investment doesn't pose a sizable risk then you can use that money for that investment.

However, speaking from experience, most of the time the risk of that investment plus the bigger amount of the debt plus interest is just too big compared to the potential return. But do the math first before you decide.

There are small investments that you can make that can return a little bit of money that can help you reduce your debts. We'll cover debt payments in detail in book 2 of this series.

Increase Your Income

Remember that the first two funds that you need to make first are your emergency fund and your savings fund. If you can start with those two first saving a thousand dollars each then you're off to a good start.

Saving up for these funds will take a lot of discipline. One of the keys to success for these two funds to flourish is to increase your income or your cash in-flow. As you find ways to reduce your expenses, you should also find ways to increase your income.

You can take a side job or two or maybe a side job and a small investment that has a decent return, as it was mentioned earlier. You can also just work a regular 9 to 5 and then create passive income assets the rest of the day (more of that later).

Here are some passive income ideas that you can try. Note that I can't guarantee that you will succeed in any of these investments. The rule of thumb here is to study and learn more about any investments first and ***you should only invest the money that you can afford to lose***.

Best Passive Income Ideas in the Next 5 to 10 Years

Creating passive income has become the new buzzword when it comes to personal finances nowadays. Some people make it look like creating passive income is rather easy. Here's a hint from personal experience – it isn't as easy as you think.

In many instances, you will have to accept the fact that you will have to work on your passive income source or asset with little or no direct compensation. You will also have to accept the fact that you will have very little income out of it for the next 3 months to 1 year. Sometimes you will have to wait up to 5 years before you actually see sizable returns that are totally passive. And that is speaking from experience.

Now, take note that not all passive income assets will work nowadays. Things have changed since the pandemic and some business models have proven to be more resilient than others.

Here are some of the more lasting and durable investments even if there's a recession, a pandemic, or even times of war and uncertainty.

1. Real Estate

Real estate in many instances is not correlated with the stock market and indices. Even if the stock market crashes, real estate companies tend to thrive even in times of uncertainty. That is true even if the company is publicly traded.

If you have a lot of cash that you can use to invest then, invest it in real estate. One way to do it is to acquire property, develop it, and earn through rental income. Notice that it will require *a lot* of money and time to develop and promote the property. But it is a potentially stable source of monthly income.

2. Rent Out a Room, an Extra Car, or Anything You Can Spare

Related to real estate, if you don't have a lot of cash to spare but you have an extra room or even another house, you can rent it to potential customers. Just remember to follow health and safety protocols.

If you have a second car that largely just stays in the garage on most days of the week, then you can offer that for rent. Look for peer-to-peer renting sites where you can rent out pretty much anything from your lawnmower to your extra bedroom or home office space.

3. Sell an Online Course

You can create an online course or offer your tutorial services. You can create tutorial videos and use that as the principal way that you deliver the instructional content. You can teach anything from playing the guitar to how to do differential calculus. You can use your own website or another platform such as Teachable or Udemy.

4. Affiliate Marketing

This is a huge topic but in a nutshell, what it means is to market someone else's products or services in exchange for a small commission. Think along the lines of the Amazon affiliate program. You can provide your affiliate links on Facebook groups, social media channels, your blog, or even on your YouTube channel.

5. Peer to Peer Lending

A lot of people today may need to borrow money when they're in a financial crunch. You can help by joining a peer to peer lending site. You can lend money and earn interest from the money you loaned out.

6. Dividend Paying Stocks

Yes, stock markets went crashing during the recent pandemic. Yes, the stock market crashed when the economy went on a slump. However, in the long term, the stock market has prevailed for decades.

If you're in it for the long haul you can invest in stocks that pay dividends. There are companies that pay quarterly dividends to shareholders, which is one of the oldest ways to earn passive income.

7. REITs and Crowdfunded Real Estate

REITs or real estate investment trust can potentially give you returns of up to 12% of your investment. It gives you a lot of flexibility. Another option, if you still want to go for the real estate route, is to try Crowdfunded real estate. If you can only spare around $500 to $5,000, then you can get started with this type of investment.

8. High Yield Savings Account

Online banking options have opened up ways for you to earn some cash on your savings accounts. If you have some extra cash and you don't want to be actively investing your funds, you can opt for this type of investment. Look for banks that offer anything from 1.55% of interest and higher and then put in money in that account over time until you have a significant amount in savings.

9. Become a Virtual Assistant

This is not a source of passive income but at least it's a way to get another source of income. If you have accounting skills, writing skills, you can do Photoshop, you can create videos, you have a talent for photography, and others, then you can offer these services and get paid for it.

Speaking of Photoshop and photography, you can create t-shirt designs, make stock photos, vectors, and other art, and then you can sell them as stock images. You can also try

120

monetizing your YouTube channel if you are able to gain a loyal following.

Final Note: building a passive income source will take time. Don't expect to make it big on the get-go. The first step is to know your market, understand your customers, and then grow your assets. The goal here is not exactly to replace your regular nine to five job but to find a second income stream to help you grow your savings and other funds faster.

Key Takeaways

- At the core of minimalist budgeting is reducing your expenses. If you can plug all the holes in your cash flow then that will already be a significant improvement.
- Do some decluttering in your home, place of work, and in your finances as well. Find ways to reduce all your expenses. If an expense is unnecessary then consider removing it from your monthly budget.
- Turn your savings into an automatic expense and it will grow eventually. Before you spend on anything, put away money for your savings first! Place that money in a separate bank account if you

have to. Put money in there and then forget about it.

- The habit of saving money is more important than the amount you are saving.
- Use the minimum $1,000 dollar funds and then grow them
- Ensure that you have at least a savings fund and an emergency fund.
- Do not depend on only one income—find ways to increase your cash in-flow.

What You Can Do

Go over your list of expenses. You're not going to do anything about your MRCs because they are absolute essentials. This time cut out all the unnecessary expenses.

For instance, if your gym membership is a potential financial leak as it were, then cancel that membership. Follow the expense reduction tips mentioned in this chapter.

Remember that if you're in a financial crunch, the first thing you should do is to stop spending on things that don't make money. In short, plug all the leaks first.

Save up to $1,000 on your savings fund. At the same time put away some money for your emergency fund. Once you have saved for your savings fund, focus on putting away money for your emergency fund. Try to grow your EF to $1,000 as well but don't stop there. You should be adding money to both of these funds each month. Set your goal amounts for both of these funds.

Later on, you can decide to put away money for your fun fund (it doesn't have to be much), personal development fund, and others as well.

Now that you have taken out all the unnecessary expenses, find ways to increase your income. Learn more about passive income sources. Sign up for courses and training that will enable you to create a passive income.

Chapter 5: Properly Managing Emotional Spending

Robert Kiyosaki once said:

"Emotions are what make us human. Make us real. The word 'emotion' stands for energy in motion. Be truthful about your emotions, and use your mind and emotions in your favor, not against yourself."

One of the habits that you need to control in order to practice a minimalist budget is emotional spending. You may have heard from salespeople that purchases are usually emotionally driven.

And that is true.

Every purchase we ever make always has an emotion backing it up. How you use those emotions to your advantage will require some smart spending habits and minimalist guiding principles as well.

Purchases are Emotionally Driven, For the Most Part

When we purchase something, it is always a decision that is in part based on our emotions. Sometimes we use our deductive reasoning and common sense. However, in many instances, we buy things based on how we feel.

In my case, whenever I felt uninspired and unmotivated I turn to a nice warm cup of coffee to get me in the mood. Sometimes it's coffee and sometimes it's ice cream—but yes, these purchases are emotionally driven.

Examples of Emotional Spending

Some emotionally charged purchasing decisions can put you into debt. But not all of them will do that. One thing is for sure though, whenever you spend money while being driven by how you feel, you end up derailing some part of your financial plans—especially in the long term.

It is important to understand what emotional spending is in order to learn how to curb it. Here are a few examples of emotional spending to help you see the inner workings of this type of behavior.

- You go out to dinner or to some fancy place to treat yourself after working hard all day. It can sometimes be followed by karaoke, theater, or maybe the movies. The usual excuse is that you deserve all of that because you have been working so hard. We think that it's okay to always splurge during these occasions.

- Whenever I get stressed at work, and my supervisor tends to micromanage things in the office, I feel unhappy and as a way to break away from all of that stress I go to one of my favorite bars and I get myself some pick-me-up. It doesn't matter how expensive the drinks and the food were—I wanted to feel better and so I deserved that little reward.

- Some people feel unhappy about how they look. They can't accept the person they see in the mirror so they give themselves a really expensive makeover. They would buy a fancy new outfit, get their hair done, and maybe even go to the spa for a really nice treatment.

After looking at those examples, do you see any kind of behavioral pattern? The common denominator in all of those decisions is that the purchases were driven by very powerful emotions.

Note that a decision based heavily on any emotion may make you feel good—it's a treat, right? Spending your hard-earned money is a sure-fire way to get some instant happiness and contentment—after all, you deserved it.

That's our usual excuse. In many instances, when our decisions are clouded by our emotions we tend to make a lot of unnecessary expenses. We may even have a budget in place—that also goes out the window the moment we spend money emotionally.

Confront Your Feelings

If you followed the little exercise we did earlier, you will notice that the first thing you have to do to avoid emotional spending is to identify and be aware of the emotions that trigger you into a spending habit.

This is a crucial step in the entire process. If you can identify, call out, and confront these feelings then you can stop yourself. It gives you a fighting chance since you are given a moment to decide whether to give in to the said emotions or not.

Understanding why you spend your hard-earned money in certain ways will help you regain self-control. Once you become aware of these emotional triggers, you can move on to the rest of the steps to overcome emotional spending.

Identify What Triggers These Emotions

Emotions aren't actually bad. They are natural and they are a part of us human beings. We are emotional creatures so it is natural to be sad, happy, angry, afraid, or even worried.

Apart from understanding and identifying our emotional triggers, we should also learn to identify the things that trigger these emotions. Just like anything else in our behaviors, our emotions are also a response to stimuli.

Stephen Covey once said that in between a stimulus and response there is a space called your freedom to choose. There is always that moment when you can decide how you can react to certain stimuli.

The more you become aware of that moment in between stimuli and response, the more empowered you become to choose even how you feel towards something. That is how people with a lot of will power are able to choose to be happy despite all the negative things that happen to them.

They do not react to things anymore. Instead, they choose how to act. In short, they become proactive instead of just being reactive. So, how do you do that?

Start small.

Identify your emotional triggers; they can be anything such as:

- The weather
- Your ex
- The news
- Certain coworkers
- Your boss
- Traffic
- Your loved ones
- Your pets
- Your kids
- Your spouse
- Scenic environment
- Music
- A religious sermon
- Sunrise
- Sunset
- A movie

- A book you might have read
- Lines of poetry
- Food
- Looking at the latest eBay offers
- Certain drinks
- Walking around malls
- The smell of cigarettes
- The taste of wine
- Browsing items on Amazon
- The smell of coffee
- A ton of other stuff

Now that you know your triggers, it's time to decide what you're going to do about them. For instance, if you find it difficult to stop yourself from buying something when you're meandering around malls, then you should spend less time in malls.

That way you don't get tempted to buy something as much. Next time you go to a mall, you have to do it purposefully and mindfully. Go there with a set plan and a specific item to buy. Get in, buy whatever you have to, and then get out.

Notice that you will get tempted to buy something from time to time but as long as you have that specific plan or item that you want to buy, you can persuade yourself to buy that item and only that item.

Sometimes you will succeed and sometimes you won't – I know, I've been there.

When you succeed:

When you succeed at overcoming emotional spending then you can congratulate yourself for a job well done.

If you don't succeed:

However, during the times when you give in to the enticement and go on an unplanned shopping spree, take a moment to forgive yourself. The best you can do at the moment is to make full use of the things you purchased.

After that, you will have to do one of the first steps in minimalist living—**decluttering**. So, how do you do that?

1. Go through the stuff you bought
2. Identify the things that are actually product duplicates of things that you already have. For example, let's say you already have a pair of running shoes but you bought a new one because there was a sale—you bought it impulsively.
3. Decide which will you keep and which one you will give away or sell. Using our current example, decide whether you want to keep the old pair of running

shoes or the new pair you recently
bought.

4. Classify the items you purchased. Identify
    the items that bring value to your life.
    Identify the things that are nice to have
    but aren't really essential.
5. Keep the items that are essential and that
    give value to your life. The rest should
    either be sold or given away to charity.
6. Repeat the said steps for all of the items
    that you bought on a whim and all other
    unplanned purchases.

Unsubscribe from Email Product Offers/Unnecessary Mailing Lists

It is no secret that we all get a lot of product
offers through our emails. A lot of them come
from mailing lists that we subscribed to.
Sometimes the emails come from our favorite
clothing store, some from Amazon Prime, some
from training or education programs that
subscribed to, and many more.

Here's a good question to ask yourself: do you
really need to see all those products offers?

There is a good chance that you may have seen a
product or email offer that you just can't resist.

They're giving 99% off on your next purchase? That is an offer you just can't refuse, right?

But they have a money-back guarantee.

Well, the guarantee is only as good as the guy behind it. Some guarantees really count for nothing if the one giving it to you isn't reliable. Take note that a lot of these offers are for products and services that you don't really need. Sometimes you just signed up for that mailing list simply because it looked like a nice thing to have when you clicked on the landing page.

The emails that these people send you are designed to entice you to buy something. All it takes is one carefully crafted offer with great copywriting to make you buy whatever it is they're selling.

The promotion will seem too good to pass off and next thing you know you're already emotionally driven to pull out your credit card and put that thing in your shopping cart.

To effectively limit any kind of temptation, you should just unsubscribe from the mailing list. Evaluate every email that you get. If it is about something that you don't really need then scroll all the way to the bottom of that email and hit "unsubscribe." Follow the prompts and have your email taken off that list.

There are, however, some offers that are worth it. It could be offers from the school that you are attending—or your kid's school. They may send you newsletters once a month. Take advantage of those offers especially if they save you money or give your child a better education.

Turn Notifications Off on Your Phone

Another source of enticement to buy something out of sheer emotion is through the notifications that you get from your phone. These aren't just ad walls that show up on your screen while you're using an app.

They're little pop-ups and notification sounds that prompt you to open your phone and check out what's on display. Sometimes they're just harmless app notifications like updates that you need to install or maybe a game event or something.

However, sometimes those notifications would be limited offers that will expire at the end of the day. Take note of the two key points of these notifications:

- There is scarcity involved—they say it is a limited offer which means they might not offer it again.
- There is a time limit—you can only use it within a certain period of time

They create an emotional response—urgency.

There is an urgency for you to make that purchase now. That is actually a marketing technique that appeals to your emotions and twists your psyche.

If you want to steer clear of these consumer traps, then do yourself a favor and turn off the notifications on your phone. You may want to leave some of the essentials like maybe a few games and maybe fitness apps and the other apps that actually benefit you.

Create a Budget for All Types of Unnecessary/Unplanned Spending

Do you remember the Fun Fund that we talked about in the previous chapter? This is what it is for. You need to set aside money for things that are fun. Your Fun Fund can be used for any unnecessary or unplanned spending.

With a Fun Fund in place, you have legroom for emotional spending and you put a cap or spending limit for it as well.

If there is anything that I have learned from my practice of minimalism and minimalist budgeting, it is this:

We are human and we give in from time to time

You may have set up the best minimalist budget that works very well for you. However, regardless of how effective it is, you still end up buying things while you're emotionally driven.

That happens to the best of us from time to time. Expect to fail at it one time or another. And it's okay. As the great Alexander Pope once said: "To err is human, to forgive divine."

So practice divinity—forgive yourself every time you give in to enticements and do some emotional spending.

But there is another thing you can do—and this one is a more advantageous strategy. Prepare a budget for unplanned expenses (aka your Fun Fund).

I always keep an extra $300 in my wallet. It's always tucked in a different part of my wallet. That's the money I use for unplanned expenses. Having that budget is a lifesaver for the following reasons:

- If you have that budget you don't overspend even if you're making an unplanned expense. It keeps your finances virtually splurge-proof. However, honestly speaking based on actual experience, it works most of the time—but sometimes I have to admit I do give-in still and go beyond $300).

- The amount is limited and it will make you think twice about that upcoming emotionally driven expense—this works especially if it is a really huge expenditure.
- It reduces the guilt you feel after you have made the purchase. You had a budget for that unplanned expense so you don't really need to beat yourself up when you do give in to your impulses.
- You keep your credit card out of the loop when it comes to unplanned expenses.

When You Are Out Shopping, Keep Your Credit Card in the Car (or at Home)

I don't really keep my credit card at home because there are times when I really need to make online purchases or use my credit card to pay for certain essentials. So what I do is I keep the credit card in the glove compartment of my car.

But if you're comfortable with the idea, then you should keep your credit card at home when you go out shopping. That means you should also bring enough cash and use that amount as your spending limit.

This rule applies to anyone who is more inclined to shop using their credit card than with cash. In such a case, using cash for shopping will help you become more mindful of your spending—which is the actual point of this rule of thumb.

Following this rule will also reduce the amount of temptation that you will feel and it will help you bring down your chances of overspending.

Apply the 24 Hour Rule

If you feel that the urge to buy something is so strong that you are having a hard time stopping yourself, then remember this rule—use it as a last resort when your emotions are high.

The rule is as follows:

Tell yourself, and keep telling yourself until you walk away from the store, that you will buy that thing tomorrow. Keep telling that to yourself until you are convinced that you can at least wait that long before you go and buy that thing.

The idea is to sleep over it. You can also apply this to any rash or hurried decisions that you are prone to make.

Applying this rule will give you a fresh start on things. You may even develop a new perspective about that purchase once you have time to let your emotions settle down.

You can also think of it as a way to practice ***delayed gratification***—in a way it is that rule applied to purchases and your expenses.

What is Delayed Gratification/Delay of Gratification?

Delay of gratification (also referred to as delayed gratification) refers to the practice of resisting any impulse to take immediate action to obtain an immediate reward. People delay immediate gratification in the hopes of getting a better and even more valuable reward in the future.

According to Ilene Cohen, a psychotherapist in Barry University's Department of Counseling, today's cultural norms encourage people to use what she calls "band aid" solutions to our experiences.

These band-aid solutions she is referring to are temporary comforts that we seek every time we encounter difficulties or are nudged into action by what we see, feel and experience.

Delaying gratification improves our emotional intelligence, increases our tolerance, and it increases our self-motivation. If you want to obtain more self-control and become a much better person than you are now, then exercising delayed gratification will allow you to develop these very fine qualities.

The Stanford University Marshmallow Experiment

There is a good chance that you have heard of the marshmallow experiment that was conducted back in 1972. It was conducted by researchers from Stanford University headed by Walter Mischel. Here is the gist of that experiment:

Children were placed in a room one at a time and were given very easy instructions. An adult left a plate with one marshmallow in it. Each child was told that if they could wait for 15 minutes—that was until the grown-up came back—that they would be given two marshmallows instead of one.

Of course, some kids were able to wait while others weren't. Researchers monitored the growth of these children. They found out that those who were able to wait for the second marshmallow had a higher emotional quotient and were less likely to have any kind of behavioral problems.

They were also found to have higher levels of self-motivation and they got better grades in school. They grew up to be more dependable people and are better at impulse control. Practicing delayed gratification contributes greatly to one's personal happiness and it is one of the traits of highly successful and effective individuals.

The good news is that you can catch up even if you lived your life instantly gratifying one impulse after another. You can grow your self-control and imbue yourself with qualities that will contribute to your life-long success.

You can practice it using the 24-hour rule.

Whenever you feel the impulse or the urge to buy something, tell yourself that you should sleep on it. Wait for 24 hours. Delaying that instant gratification for 24 hours will improve your ability to control your impulses.

By waiting for 24 hours more you may even find better deals than the one that you found. It will not only improve your ability to control impulsive buying, but it might also save you a good deal of money.

After 24 hours if you still feel like you should buy the item then go ahead. At least you have practiced a level of self-control and you have already given it some thought.

Increasing Your Ability to Delay Gratification

Some people can apply the 24-hour rule with no problems at all. Some can only hold off for a few hours. And there are those who can put off buying things for longer than one day.

Whether you can delay gratification for 8 hours or up to a full day, there are strategies that you can apply to help you improve your impulse control. Consider the following suggestions:

- ***Practice Mindfulness***

Practicing mindfulness allows you to get out of that autopilot mode of thinking. The more aware of your thoughts and intentions are, the less likely you will buy things out of sheer impulse.

Next time you feel the enticement to purchase something that you never planned to purchase, pause, and take 5 minutes to be with yourself. It can be in the bathroom, a private cubicle, or any other place where you can be alone with your thoughts.

Once you're in that private space, take a minute to breathe in and out slowly. Take really deep breaths. Pay attention to how the air goes in and out of your lungs. Think about how each breath makes you feel.

Next, allow your thoughts and feelings to center on buying that item. Don't try to convince yourself that you should buy it or not. Just pay attention to how you are feeling about that purchase.

Does it make you anxious? Do you feel excited about it? Are there any guilty thoughts and feelings associated with it?

Remember that you shouldn't make any judgments. Just pay attention and observe your feelings.

Keep observing and then notice that the intensity of that feeling or urge to buy is so strong at first. It feels as if you are truly compelled. However, don't give in just yet, just observe your feelings.

Breathe in and breathe out.

Notice that as you wait and observe, taking those slow deep breaths, the feeling and urge slowly dissipates. The feelings arise and then they fade. Keep at it and just observe the feelings, thoughts, and memories.

Breathe in and breathe out.

At the end of these five minutes, notice that the urge isn't that strong anymore. You can now make a conscious choice that is not loaded by emotions. Now you can choose whether you really want to buy that item or not.

- ***Using Your Strengths***

One way to practice delayed gratification is to anchor your behavior to one of your strengths. It's a method of self-regulation using one of your core strengths to lift you up and move you forward.

Here's an example.

If emotional and impulsive spending is one of your strengths but your love and concern for your family is one of your well-considered strengths, then you can use that strength to overcome an inherent weakness.

Some people call this as towing self-regulation. Each time you are tempted to spend money out of sheer impulse and emotion, take a moment to remember your core strength. You can do that by saying to yourself:

"I love my family too much to buy this thing right now."

Note that this same tactic can be used for any weakness that you would like to overcome.

Here are specific steps that you can take to tow a weakness using one of your core strengths:

1. Choose a strength you want to gain or a weakness you would like to overcome. In this case, you will want to prevent emotional/impulsive spending.
2. Create a visual or physical cue. It can be thought of like a special moment with your spouse and/or family that really meant a lot to you. You may also use things like a watch, bracelet, necklace, etc. that was given to you by your spouse/family.
3. Make it a habit to come back to that thought or touch/use that item first thing in the morning. Let it be a reminder to you. Throughout the day take a break or a moment to go back to that thought or object (e.g. if it is a bracelet, then touch that bracelet with your hand feeling its physical weight and recalling your emotional attachment to it and the person who gave it to you).
4. Make this a daily routine. It will be difficult at first but it can be done.
5. Whenever you are tempted to spend something outside of your budget then go back to that routine. Remind yourself of that love for your spouse/family

insomuch that you will choose them over that expense. You can also tell yourself that "I love my family too much to buy this thing right now."

6. Give yourself a reward after overcoming that temptation. It can be anything from a five-minute break, calling your wife to tell her that you love her, spending time with your kids, etc. Let the reward reinforce the strength that you have selected.

Remember that the point of using delayed gratification is to delay that unwanted or unplanned expense long enough for you to regain your composure and self-control. At the end of the exercise of delaying gratification, you can decide whether you want to buy that item after all or just purchase something that is planned or an item that is of better quality.

Identify Your Intentions

Every time you feel like you're compelled to buy something that you didn't plan to buy, ask yourself this question: "why do I want to buy this thing?"

Here's another thing you can ask yourself to get you aligned with your actual intentions. When you walk into a store and then you see something that piques your interest, ask yourself: "Is this what I am supposed to buy here?"

If the answer to that question is yes then go buy it. If not, then no, don't buy it.

The Affordability Acid Test

Here is a piece of advice from an Asian millionaire that he used when he was still totally broke and working his way towards his first 1 million dollars. Every time he is enticed to buy something he would ask if he could afford that item.

Of course, you can rationalize your way out of that question, so he devised this simple mathematical formula to determine the actual value of the item and its impact on his already diminished budget at the time.

He was a man of numbers and since numbers don't lie, this method was pretty effective at staving off any temptation to purchase something that you didn't really intend to buy.

He would take the item and hold it in his hand—if possible. He would examine it and check the price tag. After seeing the price tag, he would then do a little bit of math. He would do it this way:

- Let's say he was looking at a Breville juicer. The price tag says it is around $150.
- He would then multiply that figure by 3. Now its actual cost to his budget would be $450.
- He would then decide if the cost to his budget would be too much. In this case and at that point in time, it was too much. He just couldn't afford to lose $450 in his budget then because there were a lot of other bills he had to pay.
- That way he was able to decide, based on the cost to his current budget, that he couldn't afford the item.
- Using the same formula, he would go to a coffee shop. He ordered a $1 burger and it comes with a free drink and sides. He would multiply that by 3, and then he would get $3 for a burger, drink, and sides.
- That was a good deal given the cost to his budget, so he bought it.
- It was a frugal way to start his way up in the money game but by being strict with this formula he was able to stave off a lot

of unnecessary spending and create a nest egg that he would later use to fund a minimum of seven business enterprises.

It worked for him, I tried it, and it worked for me as well. You ought to try this one too especially if your mind is easily captivated by numbers.

Work with Accountability Partners

Get help from friends, family, a mentor, or anyone with whom you can confide with regards to your finances. It's not always easy to talk about the condition of your finances with someone so choose your accountability partners wisely.

You may want to limit this to your close friends and family. Let them know what you're curbing bad spending habits. Ask for their permission if you can call or contact them next time you feel like you're urged to spend money is way too much to handle.

They should be the ones to remind you of your goals, give you moral support, and help you make the right decisions (i.e. talk you out of that unnecessary expense). Your accountability partners don't need to be financial experts or people who have impeccable financial track records.

In fact, they don't need to be successful with their finances either. Their role is simply to be a listening ear and be someone who can give you moral support when the intensity of the enticements becomes way too much.

Use an Avoidance Plan Worksheet

An avoidance plan is a simple way to help you identify behaviors that you need to change, your triggers, and how you plan to overcome these challenges. It looks something like this:

Behavior You Want to Change
1. Habitually buying $4 lattes in the morning 2. Buying out of impulse at the mall 3. Ordering stuff online even if I didn't plan on buying it 4. Ordering extras during lunch (even if I'm not that hungry)
What Triggers These Behaviors?
1. Lunchtime 2. Rainy weather 3. Going through the mall to get a taxi

4. Email offers
5. My coworker who stresses me a lot
6. The smell of great coffee on my way to work

How Do I Plan to Avoid Them?

1. Pack my lunch beforehand
2. Get a cab on a different street or as soon as I leave the office
3. Sign out of all email lists
4. Play upbeat and uplifting music
5. Avoid that coworker as much as possible
6. Bring my own coffee to work

My Success List

1. I was able to avoid buying coffee for a week
2. I only grabbed a cookie for dessert last time I had lunch (didn't overspend)
3. Skipped the mall for a week
4. Didn't order anything from Amazon for a month

Your avoidance plan worksheet doesn't have to look like the one above. But it should at least have a list of spending habits that you want to get rid of, the triggers that signal the enticement, your action plan, and a list of victories and successes that you have achieved regardless of how big or small they are.

You don't have to make your avoidance worksheet look fancy or anything. You can even just write it down in your journal/diary. That way you can come back to it and see how far you have progressed and what problems you have encountered along the way.

Remember that this is merely a tool to give you a bird's eye view of the financial issues that you are facing. When used correctly, it can help you follow a minimalist budget and make you a more disciplined person.

Use Alternative Activities

Using alternative activities allow you to break the usual routines that may be causing you to fall into a spending trap. These activities can be anything from a walk in the park, playing mini-golf, swimming in a pool, cleaning your garage, or video messaging long lost friends.

Alternative activities should be something that you don't do a lot but you should have done them many times enough to ensure that they are things that you enjoy doing. It doesn't have to be an expensive activity. A simple afternoon jog just to break a sweat or listening to old school favorite music can work just fine.

The important thing is that these activities can help you get your mind off of buying stuff unnecessarily. Choose activities that rejuvenate your mood—things that allow you to rekindle

152

hope and inspire you well enough to see that you
can do it despite the shortcomings you may have
had in life.

Key Takeaways

- Spending money is more about your
  emotions than rational decision making.

- Sure you are cutting back on your
  spending–but it's very easy to fall into the
  same spending traps you fell for in past.
  During such times, learn to forgive
  yourself.

- The first step to controlling emotional
  spending is by identifying your spending
  triggers

- Create a fun fund and stick to that
  amount no matter what

- Practice the 24-hour rule as well as
  delayed gratification

What You Can Do

Identify what your spending triggers are.
Practice mindfulness and live in the moment so
that you become more aware of the things that
trigger you into spending unnecessarily.

Make use of the Fun Fund. In case you're really tempted to spend more than you planned, use the affordability acid test. Use the avoidance plan worksheet.

Chapter 6: Paying Off Debt and Being Liability Free

"If you're having money problems, the first thing you should do is to quit spending on ALL things that don't produce money"

(Some meme on the internet)

Debt is something that haunts us all—including minimalists. In fact, some people switch to a minimalist budget because they want to get out of debt.

One of the biggest problems that people face today is debt. You can't have complete financial freedom if you are still bogged down by large debts. You can't implement a minimalist budget and live a completely minimalist lifestyle if you are still being hounded by large amounts of debt.

Note that debt, credit scores, and all the details on how to pay it off is actually covered in full detail in book 2 of this series. In this chapter, we will only cover the ***very basics*** of debt and debt settlement as a soft introduction to book 2.

What is Debt?

Debt is the act of borrowing money from another person or financial entity. Every time you borrow funds from your friends, the bank, or your mom, you incur debt. It is your obligation to return those funds because simply put, they're not yours.

Some of the most common debts include money you borrowed to purchase a car, a house, or any other large item that has a cost that is too big for an entire month's salary to cover. Paying for your education is also a huge debt as well as any unplanned medical expenses.

Those are large amounts of debt and you often have to pay them regularly each month with interest. However, the most common (i.e. most prevalent) type of debt that a lot of people are having a difficult time paying for is none other than credit card debt. According to the Federal Reserve, back in 2019, the total credit card debt in America totaled $930 billion—the highest we have had so far.

That's just the national credit card debt. It doesn't include student loans, mortgage, and other debts that people have to pay for. Again, the Federal Reserve estimates that the national household debt is at $14.27 trillion. Some financial experts label national household debt as a kind of epidemic.

Do Minimalists Incur Debt?

Of course, they do. However, they manage them to the best of their ability and with prudence. A lot of them manage their debt so well that they don't lose sleep over it. If you can sleep soundly at night even though you have some form of debt, then you're in good shape—financially speaking.

However, if you're just starting out on your journey towards a minimalist budget and you have debts to pay, then you will have to use a systematic strategy to be debt-free.

Start with a Paradigm Shift

Yes, it's back to a paradigm shift first. I am a firm believer in changing things inside-out. You can't change your financial outlook without taking a good look at what really makes you tick on the inside.

The funny thing is that everyone believes that debt is a huge problem in many parts of the world yet very little action is being done about it. Everyone will tell you that it is some kind of universal problem—no one's going to deny that. However, the sad part is that everyone also believes that debt is a normal part of life. They seem to have surrendered to that notion.

And that is where you should start.

It's something that you should be familiar with right now since we have talked about paradigm shifts several times in this book. I always recommend dealing with finances from within first and then moving outward.

You can't just create and follow a debt payment plan without shifting your point of view. Sure, you may implement a successful campaign against your big debts, but if you still haven't changed your thought patterns, habits, and attitudes toward debt, guess what happens? You will still incur new debt and maybe find yourself back in the same hole of a debt-filled life all over again.

Remember that debt robs you of your future. It takes away your capability to grab opportunities that could have made you financially free. In fact, some people could have made very strategic investments but weren't able to do so because they were still stuck paying off their debt.

It's not just the original amount of the debt that is holding you back—the interest that comes with that debt is like a chain that won't let you go. Sometimes the interests on those debts are insane.

If your debt sounds like a mess then it probably truly—horribly is, in fact, a mess.

When Do You Start Paying Off Debt?

Here's a fact, you can't even dream of paying off your debt if you're not current on all your bills. You need to work on that first. If you focus on debt and don't pay your power bill and other utilities, then you'll end up with no electricity, or worse, no roof over your head.

The first place to start is being current on all your bills. That means if you need to take a second job, a third, and even a side hustle or small business on the side; then do it. Remember that your goal should first be to increase your cash in-flow.

Once you have that done and you're paying off your bills on time, your next goal is to work on saving up some kind of emergency fund. As a bit of a review, how much of an emergency fund should you start with as your goal again? The answer is that you should start with a goal of $1,000 for your emergency fund.

After you increase your cash flow, get current on all your monthly bills, and have saved up some kind of emergency fund, then you should start snow-balling your debt as it were.

Good Debt vs. Bad Debt

If you have ever been in debt before, you would think that it is nothing more than just a really bad experience. It's a harrowing experience and it is one that will cause you a lot of stress—especially when the debt collectors come knocking at your door.

However, you ought to know that there are two kinds of debt. Debt can be classified into two different types:

- Good debt
- Bad debt

You may have heard the saying "it takes money to make money." In the case of the finances of many folks—low income to middle-class earners—then sometimes it is necessary to have debt just to ensure that you will have something better in the future.

Now, how does that work?

You need to get good debt. Good debt is defined as any money that you owe that can help you

160

increase your income and build your wealth over time. On the other hand, there are debts that you should avoid.

These debts are called bad debts. Bad debts are any kind of consumer debts that do not improve your financial situation. In other words, they are debts that you incur that don't allow you to bring in more money now or in the near future.

In short, good debt is money that you borrow that you use now so you can make more money at the moment or in the near future. Bad debt is any kind of debt that doesn't help you bring in more money.

With that in mind, look at the following list and try to see if you can classify which of these debts are good debts and which ones are bad debts.

- Student loans
- Government debt (e.g. IRS debt)
- Personal loans
- Payday loans
- Home equity loans
- Medical debt
- Credit card debt
- Car loans
- Student loans

In my case, the biggest debts that I have ever incurred are mortgage, student loans, credit card debt, and a car loan. Examples of good debt are student loans or any kind of training or college education.

Loans for small business owners are also a form of good debt. Real estate or homeownership is also another example of good debt. Credit card debt or any kind of commercial debt is usually classified as a bad debt. Loans you make to buy clothes, cars, and other unessential items are categorized as bad debt.

What About Power and Other Utilities?

You have monthly bills like water, phone bills, electricity, gas, and other utilities, right? Sometimes you may be behind in the rent or other similar things. Remember that they aren't supposed to be classified as regular debt. Technically they're just monthly recurring expenses.

The same is true for other things like costs for childcare, groceries, taxes, and insurance. They're your normal month-to-month expenses that should be part of your budget. But sometimes how you decide to pay for these monthly recurring costs can convert these regular expenses into actual debts.

Let's say you decided this month to use your credit card to pay for your car registration, groceries, and your electric and water bill. Sure, it's a way to extend the time so you don't have to produce cash immediately. Maybe you didn't have enough money at the time—you didn't watch your cash flow as you should have.

Doing it once maybe a good excuse. You can forgive yourself. But if you do that habitually, i.e. it becomes something you do month to month, then don't be surprised to find yourself one day with a mountain of credit card debt.

> **TIP:** the goal in debt management is to help you keep out of debt. The more debt-free you are the better off your budget will be. Not to mention the fact that you will have more peace of mind if you don't have very little debt (or no debt) to worry about. A debt is still a debt, good or bad.

Borrowing Money for Investments

Some people call this practice as leveraging. You borrow money at a low-interest rate. The idea is to invest that money in an investment that has a higher rate of interest than that of the rate of interest that you had for your loan. An example of this is a margin account.

Now, this sounds like a great idea, right? It's what you don't see that will get you. I only recommend this idea to the truly experienced entrepreneur who knows how to manage risks.

There are numerous risks involved in this kind of debt. And here's another rule of thumb that you should keep in mind:

Invest only the money that you are prepared to lose

You can lose a significant amount of money if you use this strategy. Ask yourself, can your finances absorb that amount of loss (i.e. the amount of money you borrowed) in case your investment goes south?

If you don't have an emergency fund, you don't have multiple income streams, and you don't have an actual investment fund (we talked about this in a previous chapter, remember?) then this strategy of leveraging money is not a good idea—for now at least. Consider it as a kind of bad debt—for now, that is.

Is Mortgage Good Debt or Bad Debt?

If you ask some financial advisors, they will tell you that a home equity loan is a form of good debt. They will even say that it is one of the safest debts that you will ever incur. But, just like borrowing money for investments, there are certain conditions that can make it a form of good debt or bad debt.

Consider the following:

164

- If your payments for your home loan doesn't go higher than 25% of your take-home pay each month, then that is a good debt
- If the loan has a term of 15 years and it has a fixed rate then it is a good debt
- If you are offered an ARM or adjustable-rate mortgage, then it is a bad debt

Face to Face with the Truth

Here's a little exercise that I have done before that was able to awaken me to my senses. Sometimes you won't understand how dire your circumstances are until you do the math behind it.

What's the exercise? It's fairly simple. All you have to do is to add up all of your debt and make a grand total. It's not going to be fun and it's not going to be pretty. For some, like me, the grand sum of it all will even be scary.

The little excuses I made about paying it all off little by little were nothing more than just band-aid excuses simply because I couldn't see the whole picture. However, I have found out that you will never push yourself or commit yourself to resolve your debt until you come face to face with the ugly truth—you have a huge amount of debt that you are obligated to pay.

Do This Now:

So, here's what you should do. Grab a sheet of paper and a pen. Make a list of every debt you owe. You can put them into different columns and groups. One group should be your good debts and the other will be your bad debt.

For some, this will be an undesirable experience but think of it as a bitter pill that will make you feel better in the end.

After completing that list, add up all the good debt and then add up all the bad debt. And then make a grand total of all your debts at the bottom of the sheet.

Take a moment to look at that number.

For some, it will be quite an overwhelming figure. In my case, I couldn't believe how much debt I ended up owing. But it was a start—the start of my commitment to managing my finances better.

Now, if you are anything like me, you're going to scratch your head and ask yourself "How in the world am I going to be able to pay for all of that?"

The Do's and Don'ts of Debt Payment

The good news is that there are debt payment strategies that you can use. Take note that we will cover the entire subject of debt payment and how it impacts your credit scores and your finances in book two.

What we'll go over in this chapter are only the very basic strategies that you can implement to help you manage your debt. Let's begin with the debt payment strategies that you should avoid.

We all know that debt payment is not an easy task. However, you will find that there are people who will claim to have a strategy that can make your debts disappear fast. It sounds too good to be true, right? That's because it is too good to be true.

Here are four debt payment strategies that some people will say will make your debt payments faster and easier, but they just don't work.

1. Debt Consolidation

One of the debt payment strategies that might hear a lot of people are talking about is debt consolidation. Simply put, this means that you will put all of your debts into one account so that

you will consolidate them all into a single
payment.

What you will essentially be getting is a loan that
will be used to pay for all your existing debt. You
will then have to pay this consolidated account
but at a lower interest rate. Now, wouldn't that
sound great?

However, there are two big reasons why this
strategy isn't a good idea. First off, that low-
interest rate isn't going to stay low for the entire
duration of this loan. This low-interest rate will
eventually go up as you progress in your
payments. It's not going to stay low forever—
someone has to make money when they pay for
your loan.

The other reason why this strategy isn't a good
idea is that you will end up staying in debt much
longer. What you're doing is stretching the debt
over a longer period of time. In essence, you will
be allowing yourself to experience the
excruciating burden of making debt payments
for many more years.

The goal is to pay your debt as fast as you can so
that you won't have to suffer that long and not to
allow the interest to accrue over time. Debt
consolidation is a bad deal if you consider its
long-term effects.

2. Borrowing from Your 401(k)

Getting a 401(k) loan is a terrible idea. Some people might suggest this to you but this is a really bad idea. What is your 401(k) for in the first place? Remember that this is your investment in your retirement. If you take away from it now, you are setting yourself up for a lot of problems in the future.

Apart from that, you are putting yourself at a huge risk. When you withdraw money from your 401(k), you can get charged with penalties. Your withdrawal will also be subject to taxes and fees. That will greatly reduce the amounts that you have invested and you don't want that since on top of the reduced amount, you will also have to deal with inflation in the future.

3. Work with Debt Settlement Companies

There may be times when you will be approached by debt settlement companies. Here's a quick tip when you get that call—don't settle with them. They will promise that they can negotiate with your creditor and haggle for a lower amount of money for you to pay.

However, they can seldom be able to negotiate for a lower amount. They will just take what you can pay, collect their fees, and then leave you with your debt not even fully paid. Their goal is to collect their fees and make their living—that's it.

4. Home Equity Line of Credit

Some might suggest that you try getting a home equity line of credit (HELOC). This idea is just as bad as the other three we mentioned earlier. In fact, it might even be worse. What a HELOC essentially is that it is a loan. You are using credit to pay for your debt. You're going into debt to pay for a previous debt. In simple terms, you're making a mistake to fix a previous mistake.

As you might have already guessed, it's not going to work. With this strategy, you are using your house as your collateral. If you can't pay back this loan in time you will risk losing your home. The moral of the story here is that it isn't a good idea to use debt to pay for a debt.

Paying for Your Debts the Smart Way

So, what can you do to pay for your debts and be rid of them permanently? My good friend quoted Dave Ramsey, he's such a big Ramsey fan, and said: "You need to increase your shovel-to-hole-ratio."

I felt dumbstruck after I heard that. It made so much sense.

I dug myself into a very deep hole, to begin with by going into debt. What I need to do is to increase my proverbial shovel to fill up that hole. That means I need to increase my cash flow so that I would have more money to pay for my debts.

I also need to let go of certain things—like that second car that I didn't really need.

If you remember the quote I mentioned at the beginning of this chapter, it goes like this:

"If you're having money problems, the first thing you should do is to quit spending on ALL things that don't produce money"

That's one of the two things you should do. The first is to plug all the leaks in your finances. That's where your minimalist budget comes in handy. You minimize everything—including your expenses.

And then you increase your cash flow. Find other sources of income. You can get another job, do a side hustle, and maybe make an active investment in a business that will bring you passive income.

The next step is to use a sound debt payment strategy. And in line with that, I would like to suggest two proven debt payment strategies for you.

Snowball vs. Avalanche

Paying off your debt may seem overwhelming, but if you use a sound debt-repayment strategy, the burden of paying it off will be made easier. You just need the right attitude, mindset, and proper behavior towards that debt.

The two popular debt repayment methods are the debt avalanche and the debt snowball method. We'll go over the details of each method and at the end of it, you get to decide which debt reduction method is the better option for you.

What is the Debt Snowball Method?

Millions of people have used the debt snowball method to pay off their debts and it has worked well for them. Remember that paying debts is not about the math but has more to do with your attitude towards paying the debt. The debt snowball method does more than just reduce your debts—it changes your behavior, it's a form of behavior modification, and for a good reason.

Why call it the "snowball" method?

Here's why—do you remember when back when you were a kid playing in the snow in your backyard? You can't just grab a huge chunk of snow and turn it into a huge ball that you can hurl at your friends or make into a snowman, right?

That kind of snowball won't do.

What you needed to do is to get a smaller amount of snow, one that could fit into your hand, and pack it tight. And then you roll it all over your yard so that it turns into a huge ball later on.

If you keep it on doing that, your ball will begin to grow bigger—faster. And it wouldn't take long for you to make a really huge snowball. Well, by that time you won't call it a "ball" anymore—it's a boulder!

That's basically how the debt snowball method works. You start small and work your way up. That means you start allotting the most amount of money to pay off your smallest debt quickly.

Once you're done paying off the smallest debt, you move on to the next smallest debt using the extra money you have (because you've paid off one debt) to pay that debt. You keep doing that until you have fully paid every single debt on your list.

> **Summary**: the debt snowball method is a method to pay off your debt where you completely pay off your smallest debt first allotting the most money into that debt. You pay the minimum on all the other debts. You then work your way up rolling

the money over and over to cover for the next succeeding debt until you have the last and biggest debt left to pay. You then use all the money that you have rolled over through the months to pay off your final debt.

Why Does the Snowball Method Work?

A lot of people would usually say that you need to get rid of the biggest debt first. It's the same principle they apply at work. They will say you should tackle the most difficult and biggest task first.

That seems like the smart thing to do, right?

Well, what happens if you do that? You end up losing steam along the way simply because paying off debts isn't fun. Would you agree? There's no reward behind that strategy. That is why when you pay off the biggest debt and the one with the biggest interest, you end up losing interest because it will feel like there's no end to the payments that you have to make.

The snowball method works because each time you pay off your smallest debts you get a sense of accomplishment—not to mention a small bump in your funds as well.

Stephen Covey once said that small victories precede bigger victories. Big things start from small things. The sense of accomplishment is also a big morale booster as well.

How to Do the Debt Snowball Method

Remember that you focus on paying off the smallest debt first when you use the snowball method. While using this debt payment method, you will still look for ways to increase your cash flow so that you can get additional funds to support your needs and also add more money that you can use to pay for your debts.

Here are the steps that you will take to do the debt snowball method:

1. Make a list of all the debts that you have to pay. You should have done this earlier if you followed the principles discussed here in this chapter. Earlier we had that face to face section where you had to make a grand total of all your debts. What you should do now is to make a new list where your debts are arranged by the amount that you should pay. The one with the smallest amount should be at the top of your list.

2. The next step is to determine the minimum amounts that you should pay for each of the debts on your list.
3. Allot specific amounts on your budget to pay for the minimum amounts.
4. Allot amounts for the different parts of your budget (e.g. bills, essentials, emergency fund, fun fund, and other recurring monthly costs).
5. Any extra cash you have left over should be allotted to the smallest debt that you have to pay.
6. Pay off the smallest debt, and then the rest of your debts.
7. You can then spend the rest of your money on the other budgeted items as well.
8. If during this process you have fully paid your smallest debt, then scratch that debt off your list and then proceed to pay the next one. Remember to roll over the funds you used to pay your previously smallest debt to pay for the new smallest debt amount.
9. Next month, repeat this process until all your debts are paid.

Snow Ball Method Example

Here's an example of how you can use the debt snowball method. Let's say this is my list of debts:

1. Personal loan = $500
2. Credit card = $2,500
3. Car loan = $6,000
4. Student loan = $15,000

What I would do is to allot part of my budget to pay for the minimum for all 4 debts on this list. I will then allot money for the other things I need for this month.

Let's say I made a $100 payment for my personal loan since that is the minimum payment for it each month. After that I have allotted money for every item on my budget, I discover that I had an extra $400 left.

Instead of celebrating—making a sacrifice this month and deferring any gratification (let's say I wanted to buy a new cellphone to replace my old iPhone)—I would then use that extra $400 to pay off my personal loan.

So, this month I would have paid for my personal loan so I scratch that off my list. Next month I have this list of debts I need to pay:

1. Credit card = $2,350

2. Car loan = $5,850
3. Student loan = $14,850

In the next month, I will use the extra $500 that I would have used to pay for the previous personal loan to pay for the credit card debt. Let's say I usually make $150 as a minimum payment for my credit card debt.

This month I will pay $650 for my credit card debt, $500 from my extra funds + $150 from my usual minimum (all of this hypothetical only, okay—big grin).

So that means in the following month I will have this much debt left:

1. Credit card = $ 1,700
2. Car loan = $ 5,700
3. Student loan = $ 14,700

As you can see, since I rolled over the money I would have used to pay for my personal loan as payment for the new smallest debt in my list (i.e. credit card) I have made a rather huge payment for that debt this month.

It might take me three more months but I would have paid for my credit card debt in full in just 5 payments instead of making roughly 17 payments to pay for the entire thing. I have paid for 2 debts on my list in 7 months instead of a year and a half.

After paying for the first debt, I felt a sense of accomplishment. And having seen that I have taken off a huge amount from my credit card debt, I get a huge confidence booster. On top of that, I was able to reduce my other debts. This raises my self-esteem and it also gives me a sense of hope that things are getting better.

In essence, I am making sacrifices now so that I can be debt-free sooner.

This confidence boost is a huge motivation for me to keep ongoing. I need to make sacrifices for at least 3 years. But that is a big trade-off. I get to pay all of my debt in 3 years instead of paying for it for almost 10 years.

What is the Debt Avalanche Method?

The debt avalanche method, as you might have guessed, is a radically different option to pay off your debts. This debt payment method is also known as debt stacking. In this method, instead of arranging your debts according to the amount of the debt, you will arrange them from the highest interest rate first to the one with the lowest interest rate last.

This is basically how we instinctively pay for our debts. So, let's say you have a student loan that is worth $15,000 that carries a 20% interest on your list. And then you have another big debt, which is your credit card debt amounting to $2,500 but with a 5% interest. Using the debt avalanche strategy, you will do all you can to pay off the student loan first.

If you use your funds to pay for a $15,000 student loan, chances are you won't have much money left for the rest of your other debts and not to mention your needs as well as your monthly bills too.

Some would suggest that you do a balance transfer of your credit card debt. That means you move your credit card debt from one bank to another. Where would you get the money to pay for the other debts and loans? Some would suggest that you should consolidate them.

The suggestions get fuzzy from one debt avalanche practitioner to the next. But one thing is clear if you have more than enough funds to pay for your $15,000 student loan, and plenty of cash to spare for your other needs, then you can do that.

Next month you have an extra $15,000 that you can use to pay for the other debts. However, a lot of folks today don't have an extra $15,000 lying around. Most of us are barely getting by.

If you have enough funds, then the debt avalanche method is a great option for you. You get to pay for your debts a lot faster that way. However, if you don't have plenty of funds coming in each month from your job, side hustle, investments, and small business, then the debt snowball method is your best option. It may be a long-haul solution but at least you have enough for everything you need and it gives you a sense of fulfillment.

If you do try the debt avalanche method, take note of this little caveat – losing a huge chunk of your bank balance (e.g. $15,000 gone in one go) can be demoralizing at some point or another. Find a huge morale booster along the way to keep you motivated to go to work and find money that you can use to pay for your remaining debts.

Key Takeaways

- Debt is the act of borrowing money from someone else. When you borrow money, you are duty-bound and legally bound to that person or financial entity. In other words, harsh as it may seem, but incurring debt is servitude.

- Now, this is something from the Bible, not that I am really religious or anything. But the good book tells us that the borrower is a slave to the lender. The moment you enter into that contract, you enter into a bond of servitude. In effect, you are working for that person you borrowed money from.

- Make sure that you are current with your MRCs first before you think about paying off debt. Find other sources of income to make ends meet.

- There are good debts and there are bad debts—but they're all still debts.

- There are good debt payment strategies and there are bad debt payment strategies—some bad strategies are even suggested by financial planners.

- The debt snowball method is still the best way to get out of debt.

What You Can Do

At this point, you ought to have found a way to generate extra income. It can come in the form of a second job, a side hustle, or a type of passive income. The important thing is to increase your shovel to hole ratio as it were.

Use the debt snowball method to pay off your debt. Go back to your financial goals and remind yourself of these goals every time you feel like debt payments are never-ending.

Use your fun fund to relieve yourself of the stress of debt payments. Hang in there. You can do this!

Conclusion

Thanks again for taking the time to go through this book from cover to cover.

It is my hope that as you followed each step that you have formulated a minimalist budget that works best for you. You should at least have started a savings fund and an emergency fund.

But most of all, it is my hope that you experienced a paradigm shift. Minimalism applied to our finances is more of an internal change first before it has any effect on the way we spend our money.

Make that internal change and then you can make a minimalist budget work best for you.

If you enjoyed this book, please take the time to leave me a review on Amazon. I appreciate your honest feedback, and it really helps me to continue producing high-quality books.